RESEARCHER ROLES & RESEARCH PARTNERSHIPS

ETHNOGRAPHER'S TOOLKIT

Edited by Jean J. Schensul, *Institute for Community Research, Hartford,* and
Margaret D. LeCompte, *School of Education, University of Colorado, Boulder*

The **Ethnographer's Toolkit** is designed with you, the novice fieldworker, in mind. In a series of seven brief books, the editors and authors of the **Toolkit** take you through the multiple, complex steps of doing ethnographic research in simple, reader-friendly language. Case studies, checklists, key points to remember, and additional resources to consult are all included to help the reader fully understand the ethnographic process. Eschewing a step-by-step formula approach, the authors are able to explain the complicated tasks and relationships that occur in the field in clear, helpful ways. Research designs, data collection techniques, analytical strategies, research collaborations, and an array of uses for ethnographic work in policy, programming, and practice are described in the volumes. The **Toolkit** is the perfect starting point for professionals in diverse professional fields including social welfare, education, health, economic development, and the arts, as well as for advanced students and experienced researchers unfamiliar with the demands of conducting good ethnography.

Summer 1999/7 volumes/paperback boxed set/0-7619-9042-9

BOOKS IN THE ETHNOGRAPHER'S TOOLKIT

1. **Designing and Conducting Ethnographic Research,** by Margaret D. Le Compte and Jean J. Schensul, 0-7619-8975-7 (paperback)

2. **Essential Ethnographic Methods: Observations, Interviews, and Questionnaires,** by Stephen L. Schensul, Jean J. Schensul, and Margaret D. LeCompte, 0-7619-9144-1 (paperback)

3. **Enhanced Ethnographic Methods: Audiovisual Techniques, Focused Group Interviews, and Elicitation Techniques,** by Jean J. Schensul, Margaret D. LeCompte, Bonnie K. Nastasi, and Stephen P. Borgatti, 0-7619-9129-8 (paperback)

4. **Mapping Social Networks, Spatial Data, and Hidden Populations,** by Jean J. Schensul, Margaret D. LeCompte, Robert T. Trotter II, Ellen K. Cromley, and Merrill Singer, 0-7619-9112-3 (paperback)

5. **Analyzing and Interpreting Ethnographic Data,** by Margaret D. LeCompte and Jean J. Schensul, 0-7619-8974-9 (paperback)

6. **Researcher Roles and Research Partnerships,** by Margaret D. LeCompte, Jean J. Schensul, Margaret R. Weeks, and Merrill Singer, 0-7619-8973-0 (paperback)

7. **Using Ethnographic Data: Interventions, Public Programming, and Public Policy,** by Jean J. Schensul, Margaret D. LeCompte, G. Alfred Hess, Jr., Bonnie K. Nastasi, Marlene J. Berg, Lynne Williamson, Jeremy Brecher, and Ruth Glasser, 0-7619-8972-2 (paperback)

RESEARCHER ROLES & RESEARCH PARTNERSHIPS

MARGARET D. LeCOMPTE
JEAN J. SCHENSUL
MARGARET R. WEEKS
MERRILL SINGER

6 ETHNOGRAPHER'S TOOLKIT

ALTAMIRA
PRESS
A Division of Sage Publications, Inc.
Walnut Creek ◆ London ◆ New Delhi

For information:

AltaMira Press
A Division of Sage Publications, Inc.
1630 North Main Street, Suite 367
Walnut Creek, CA 94596
explore@altamira.sagepub.com
http://www.altamirapress.com

SAGE Publications Ltd.
6 Bonhill Street
London EC2A 4PU
United Kingdom

SAGE Publications India Pvt. Ltd.
M-32 Market
Greater Kailash I
New Delhi 110 048 India

Printed in the United States of America

Library of Congress Cataloging-in-Publication Data

Main entry under title:

Researcher roles and research partnerships / by Margaret D. LeCompte . . . [et al.].
    p. cm. — (Ethnographer's toolkit; v. 6)
  Includes bibliographical references and index.
  ISBN 0-7619-8973-0 (alk. paper)
    1. Ethnology—Methodology. 2. Ethnology—Field work.
I. LeCompte, Margaret Diane. II. Series.
  GN345.R47 1999
  305.8'001—dc21   99-6349

Production Editor: Astrid Virding
Editorial Assistant: Nevair Kabakian
Designer/Typesetter: Janelle LeMaster
Cover Designer: Ravi Balasuriya
Cover Artists: Ed Johnetta Miller, Graciela Quiñones Rodriguez

CONTENTS

INTRODUCTION

The **Ethnographer's Toolkit** is a series of texts on how to plan, design, carry out, and use the results of applied ethnographic research. Ethnography, as an approach to research, may be unfamiliar to people accustomed to more traditional forms of research, but we believe that applied ethnography will prove not only congenial but essential to many researchers and practitioners. Many kinds of evaluative or investigative questions that arise in the course of program planning and implementation cannot be answered very well with standard research methods such as experiments or collection of quantifiable data. Often, there are no data yet to quantify or programs whose effectiveness needs to be assessed! Sometimes, the research problem to be addressed is not yet clearly identified and must be discovered. In such cases, ethnographic research provides a valid and important way to find out what *is* happening in programs and to help practitioners plan their activities.

This book series defines what ethnographic research is, when it should be used, and how it can be used to identify and solve complex social problems, especially those not readily amenable to traditional quantitative or experimental research methods alone. It is designed for educators; service professionals; professors of applied students in the fields of teaching, social and health services, communications, engineering, and business; and students working in applied field settings.

Ethnography is a peculiarly human endeavor; many of its practitioners have commented that, unlike other approaches to research, the *researcher* is the primary tool for collecting primary data. That is, as Books 1, 2, 3, and 4 of this series demonstrate, the ethnographer's principal database is amassed in the course of human interaction: direct observation; face-to-face interviewing and elicitation; audiovisual recording; and mapping the networks, times, and places in which human interactions occur. Thus, as Book 6 makes clear, the personal characteristics and activities of researchers as human beings and as scientists become salient in ways not applicable in research where the investigator can maintain more distance from the people and phenomena under study.

Book 1 of the **Ethnographer's Toolkit**, *Designing and Conducting Ethnographic Research*, defines what ethnographic research is and the predominant viewpoints or paradigms that guide ethnography. It provides the reader with an overview of research methods and design, including how to develop research questions, what to consider in setting up the mechanics of a research project, and how to devise a sampling plan. Ways of collecting and analyzing data and the ethical consideration for which ethnographers must account conclude this overall introduction to the series.

In Book 2, *Essential Ethnographic Methods*, readers are provided with an introduction to participant and nonparticipant observation; interviewing; and ethnographically informed survey research, including systematically administered structured interviews and questionnaires. These data collection strategies are fundamental to good ethnographic research. The essential methods provide ethnographers with tools to answer the principal ethnographic questions: "What's happening in this setting?" "Who is engaging in what kind of activities?" and "Why are they doing what they are doing?" Ethnographers use them to enter a field situation and obtain basic information about social structure, social events, cultural patterns, and the meanings people give to these patterns. The essential tools also permit ethnographers to learn about new situations from the perspective of insiders because they require ethnographers to become involved in the local cultural setting and to acquire their knowledge through hands-on experience.

In Book 3, *Enhanced Ethnographic Methods*, the reader adds to this basic inventory of ethnographic tools three different but important approaches to data collection, each one a complement to the essential methods presented in Book 2. These tools are audiovisual techniques, focused group interviews, and elicitation techniques. We have termed these data collection strategies "enhanced ethnographic methods" because each of them parallels and enhances a strategy first presented in Book 2.

Audiovisual techniques, which involve recording behavior and speech using electronic equipment, expand the capacity of ethnographers to observe and listen by creating a more complete and permanent record of events and speech. Focused group interviews permit ethnographers to interview more than one person at a time. Elicitation techniques allow ethnographers to quantify qualitative or perceptual data on how individuals and groups of people think about and organize perceptions of their cultural world.

It is important for the reader to recognize that, although the essential ethnographic methods described in Book 2 can be used alone, the enhanced ethnographic methods covered in Book 3 cannot, by themselves, provide a fully rounded picture of cultural life in a community, organization, work group, school, or other setting. Instead, they must be used in combination with the essential methods outlined in Book 2. Doing so adds dimensions of depth and accuracy to the cultural portrait constructed by the ethnographer.

In Book 4, *Mapping Social Networks, Spatial Data, and Hidden Populations,* we add to the enhanced methods of data collection and analysis used by ethnographers. However, the approach taken in Book 4 is informed by a somewhat different perspective on the way social life is organized in communities. Whereas the previous books focus primarily on ways of understanding cultural patterns and the interactions of individuals and groups in cultural settings, Book 4 focuses on how social networks, patterns of interaction, and uses of what we term "sociogeographic space" influence human behavior and beliefs.

Book 5, *Analyzing and Interpreting Ethnographic Data,* provides the reader with a variety of methods for transforming piles of fieldnotes, observations, audio- and videotapes, questionnaires, surveys, documents, maps, and other kinds of data into research results that help people to understand their world more fully and facilitate problem solving. Addressing both narrative and qualitative, as well as quantitative—or enumerated—data, Book 5 discusses methods for organizing, retrieving, rendering manageable, and interpreting the data collected in ethnographic research.

This book, *Researcher Roles and Research Partnerships,* is the sixth book in the series. It discusses two aspects of the researcher's life in the field. Chapter 1 approaches the roles that researchers working as individual project directors or initiators of research adopt and acquire in the course of research activities; strategies for entry and survival in the field site; how the personal, professional, and philosophical characteristics of the researcher affect his or her access to information; and the ethical responsibilities for which ethnographers are accountable in the field. Chapter 2 addresses the roles, strategies, and responsibilities of researchers who are working in, or organizing, research partnerships.

The final book in the series, *Using Ethnographic Data: Interventions, Public Programming, and Public Policy,* consists of three chapters that present general guidelines and case studies illustrating how ethnographers have used ethnographic data in planning public programs, developing and evaluating interventions, and influencing public policy.

Throughout the series, authors give examples drawn from their own work and the work of their associates. These examples and case studies present ways in which ethnographers have coped with the kinds of problems and dilemmas found in the field—and described in the series—in the course of their work and over extended periods of time.

Readers less familiar with ethnographic research will gain an introduction to basic ethnographic principles, methods, and techniques by reading Books 1, 2, 5, and 6 first, followed by other books that explore more specialized areas of research and use. Those familiar with basic ethnographic methods will find Books 3, 4, and 7 valuable in enhancing their repertoires of research methods, data collection techniques, and ways of approaching the use of ethnographic data in policy and program settings.

—Jean J. Schensul and Margaret D. LeCompte

1 ━●━●━●━

RESEARCHER ROLES

Margaret D. LeCompte

Ethnography is a peculiarly human endeavor; many of its practitioners have commented that, unlike other approaches to research, the *researcher* is the primary tool for collecting primary data. As Books 1, 2, 3, and 4 of the **Ethnographer's Toolkit** demonstrate, the ethnographer's principal database is amassed in the course of human interaction: direct observation; face-to-face interviewing and elicitation; audiovisual recording; and mapping the networks, times, and places in which human interactions occur. Thus, the personal characteristics and activities of researchers as human beings and as scientists become salient in ways not applicable in research where the investigator can maintain more distance from the people and phenomena under study. Access to the research setting, the key informants, and other participants who constitute the focus of the study depends on the appearance, presentation of self, social skills, and specific behaviors of the ethnographer in the research setting. Generally, communities and research participants are polite and will accept a wide variety of researcher characteristics, including eccentricities of clothing, speech, hair style, and even beliefs and personal

Key point   habits. However, *it is critically important for prospective researchers to learn ahead of time, or discover early on, the boundaries of acceptable behavior and lifestyle to ensure high comfort levels for both researcher and study participants.*

THE EMBEDDED CONTEXTS AND MULTIPLE ROLES OF ETHNOGRAPHIC WORK

Previous books in the **Ethnographer's Toolkit** have made it clear that ethnographic research is a complex and multifaceted process. No less complex are the multilayered and overlapping settings in which ethnographic research takes place. A good way of thinking about the context of ethnographic research is to envision it as a series of concentric circles in which smaller contexts are embedded within larger ones. Figure 1.1 illustrates such embedded contexts. Each of these contexts provides the social context for a variety of social responsibilities and obligations required of ethnographic researchers.

As Figure 1.1 indicates, the contexts in which ethnographers operate are the following:

- The *culture of the community* in which the research project is located, as well as the culture of each person involved in the project
- The *government of the country or community* in which the project is located and its associated regulations for and constraints on research
- The *network of institutions* collaborating in the design and execution of the project
- The *individual institutions or organizations* that constitute the research site
- *Small groups* that are the structural components of the site, including classrooms, work groups, friendship cliques, and social networks
- *Individual research participants*

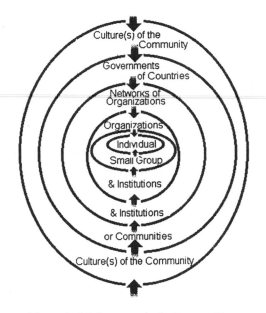

Figure 1.1. The embedded contexts[1] of ethnographic research.
SOURCE: Adapted from Cole and Griffen (1987)

Within these contexts, researchers are responsible for the following:

- Initiating, arranging, and carrying out the ongoing business of data collection and analysis during the course of the research project.
- Analyzing and interpreting the data, which means determining how the masses of raw questionnaires, observational notes, interviews, tests, maps, and a variety of other raw data sources make sense when taken as a whole.
- Helping people in the research site make sense of data in ways that not only help researchers understand them better, but result in research presentations that are meaningful to the group that requested the study in the first place.

Cross Reference: See Book 5 for an extended discussion of analysis and interpretation

These primary responsibilities of the researcher require skill in human relations and communications, all of which are needed, in turn, in order to carry out successfully a whole series of social responsibilities. These include the following:

- Taking responsibility for making and maintaining relationships with research participants, members of the research team, and staff for partnership organizations
- Solving personal problems between and among research team members, research participants, members of the research team and partnership organizations, and community institutions whose activities impinge upon the research project
- Identifying and avoiding, or extricating themselves and members of the research team from risky or dangerous situations
- Figuring out how to give feedback—and how much to give—to various players in such a way as to maintain both candor and civil relationships
- Determining what kinds of feedback will be most helpful in furthering the objectives of partnership institutions and research participants
- Developing ways to say goodbye or for attenuating the relationships and interdependencies created in the field once the project is over
- Maintaining necessary contacts at a distance once the researcher has left the field
- Serving as a spokesperson for or commentator on the events that transpired in the field once reports have been finished and the researchers' contractual obligations have ended

 Definition: A role is a position within a social structure that is defined by the obligations and responsibilities assigned by the culture to that position and the expectations that other people have for how the person occupying that role should think and behave

Key to understanding how to carry out all these responsibilities is understanding the impact of the researcher's person on the research process. The researcher's *person* is made up of two components: First is what we refer to as the "**role (or roles) of the researcher.**" The second component consists of the personal, demographic, and physical characteristics of researchers. We first discuss researcher roles.

THE ETHNOGRAPHER'S MANY ROLES

In everyday life, each of us plays multiple roles. A woman can simultaneously be a mother, daughter, employer/employee, friend, club member, sibling, lover or wife (or both), churchgoer, recipient of public assistance, former refugee, student, and immigrant. Each of these roles develops a "self" peculiar to it and framed by the responsibilities and privileges, expectations and obligations defining that role. Thus, each individual inhabits multiple roles, which in turn create multiple "identities," each of which has somewhat specialized functions and limitations.

The influence of role obligations, responsibilities, and rights can be so compelling that people may react to a person more in terms of his or her role than they do in terms of the individual's special personal characteristics. In a sense, people actually "see" roles as clearly as they see the people who inhabit those roles. Thus, when a group of teachers says, "I don't care if Mr. Smith is a nice guy; he's still the superintendent of schools!" they mean that Mr. Smith's authority over them, in his role as superintendent, mitigates his "niceness"; this causes them to *expect* him to act in an authoritative way, and it creates social distance between them and him in social interaction. Similarly, teenagers may assert, "My Mom is my best friend!" while at the same time hiding from Mom evidence of behavior of which they know that she, in her role as parent, would disapprove.

In everyday life—and particularly in western European and North American life—these discrete roles or selves each carry out their functions more or less within the confines of their particular and appropriate situation. Thus, people may compartmentalize their many roles, restricting what they communicate to others to messages appropriate for the situation. For example, some people may find it difficult to communicate intimate details about their private lives as spouses, parents, or hobbyists while at work. Others become skilled at identifying when they can cross boundaries in "normal" situations.

Ethnographic research imposes many varied identities and special role relationships on researchers during the course of their investigations. Ethnographers not only occupy the normal roles people play in everyday life, but they also acquire additional roles that are specific to their activities in the field. Some of these derive from the relationships that they form in the research site; other roles derive from their personality and appearance. In the pages that follow, we discuss the following:

- Stereotypic portrayals of scientific research and researchers
- The ethnographer's multiple roles and their origins
- The conflicts and difficulties these roles create
- What ethnographers do to enact their roles effectively
- How the multiple roles of the researcher can facilitate the conduct of ethnographic research

Confronting the Stereotype of Scientific Neutrality

Cross Reference: See Book 1, Chapter 3, for a discussion of positivism and tenets of objectivity

We begin by exploring some conventional stereotypes about science and researchers because we feel that these stereotypes still affect how even ethnographers are perceived by nonresearchers. The roots of the conventional stereotype can be found in the philosophy of positivism, which we discuss in Book 1. Although this philosophy does not apply very well to ethnographic research, its influence has affected how laypeople think about science and scientists. Conventional stereotypes still affect the reception that ethnographers receive among research participants and from institutions with which ethnographers might want to work, even though they are not true for ethnographers.

The conventional stereotype depicts researchers as solitary white males in starched laboratory coats, diligently running experiments on small mammals, mixing chemicals in laboratory test tubes, or administering tests to people in clinical settings. Occasionally, the stereotype involves a team effort. In team efforts, the lone scientist is replaced by a chief of research, authoritatively administering a hierarchically organized effort. Teams may include people with lower status than scientists, but differences between lower status participants are marked—as, for example, in a medical team that consists of a group of white men in white lab coats . . . assisted by women technicians in green lab coats. Crucial to this stereotype is a simplistic notion of the researcher's role: Find out the "truth" and report it to the awaiting community of scholars. The researcher's stance toward the people or phenomena under study is similarly simplistic: Do not get involved with the subjects, and maintain a detached and neutral stance toward results and their consequences. Most important, the conventional stereotype assumes both that researchers can control all—or at least most—of their personal biases about what the outcomes of the research would be and how the results would be used, and that any technical or procedural biases that might remain could be controlled by the research design that researchers develop.

There are many reasons why this stereotype not only does not characterize, but is inappropriate for, the kind of applied and critical ethnography described in the **Ethnographer's Toolkit**.

Limitations of the Conventional Stereotype

- Little, if any, ethnographic research takes place in controlled laboratory settings or other settings in which some measure of technical, procedural, or design control over the course of events to be studied is possible.
- The stereotype omits many steps in the research process: planning and design; assembling research teams; gaining access to the field; analyzing, debating about interpretations of, and writing up data; and disseminating results to a broad public.
- It ignores the human relationships that are crucial to the success of any ethnography.

**Cross
Reference:**
See Book 1
and the discussion
of positivism for
the origins of the
stereotype

**Cross
Reference:**
Note the
discussion of
Institutional Review
Boards in Book 1
and later in this
chapter

- It discounts the human characteristics of the researcher, including his or her personal tastes, personality, and training, which are important during problem definition, data collection, and choice of frameworks for interpretation of research results.

- It treats researchers as if it were possible for them to have no opinions or biases.

- It regards human subjects of research and their problems as objects of study, rather than as individuals whose needs, privacy, and safety must be considered.

- It gives limited consideration to the issue of the researcher's audience: when, to whom, and how results of research should be reported.

- The stereotype also does not reflect the gender, ethnic, class, occupational, and educational diversity found in the contemporary scientific community.

**Cross
Reference:**
See Book 2,
Chapters 4 and 5,
on participant
observation and
in-depth
interviewing

The conventional stereotype has been increasingly discredited, in large part because we now know that it is impossible for ethnographers to maintain the detachment called for in the stereotype; in fact, it is impossible for *any* researcher to set aside all biases, if only because some of them involve issues of which researchers are unaware or find beyond their control. It may also be unwise to attempt to remain entirely neutral, because many of the hunches or ideas that researchers have about what they observe and that they use to begin analysis and interpretation of results do, in fact, come from their own personal interests and preferences, as well as from their theoretical perspectives. Furthermore, the principal tenet of participant observation—the most important data collection strategy used by ethnographers—is that ethnographers come to understand the people whom they study *through engagement with them.* For example, people are much more likely to talk freely about their experiences if they feel that the researcher can share in and empathize with the difficulties and joys attendant to those experiences. Empathy, after all, is a critical dimension of participant observation; people being studied are much more likely to feel that the researcher's feelings of empathy are authentic if they know that the researcher has had similar experiences, as Example 1.1 demonstrates.

➤•➤•➤ **EXAMPLE 1.1**

BUILDING RAPPORT AND UNDERSTANDING BY SHARING EXPERIENCES AND ROLES

One ethnographer found that her past experience as a school administrator helped the school staff for whom she was conducting a study of school reform feel more comfortable confiding in her. She, too, they agreed, had been "in the trenches," as they were. Those confidences greatly facilitated collecting data on the difficulties and agonies of institutional change, even though some involved disclosures that were more cathartic than enlightening, and several made the ethnographer privy to information to which she was not legally entitled. During an informal conversation with the ethnographer, one frustrated school principal suddenly pulled out the records of one teacher who was suspected of sexual abuse and another who had been accused by a group of very religious parents of drug use. As confidential records, all of these documents were supposed to be closed to the ethnographer's scrutiny. "I suspect that the first teacher *might be* an abuser. And although it isn't pleasant, I know I'll have to confront him. But the second teacher is just being made the victim of parents who don't agree with her particular philosophy of teaching. She isn't a very good teacher,"—here he pulled out the teacher's evaluation record—"but she isn't an addict. The problem is, the parents who don't like her are powerful in this community." The ethnographer was left knowing information that was not relevant to her study, and was not her right to know, but about which the principal needed to talk. He chose the ethnographer as a trusted neutral confidant.

➤•➤•➤

For many years, anthropologists have argued—and more recently, critical theorists and some feminists have joined them—not only that maintaining positivistic neutrality is impossible to achieve, but that it constitutes poor research practice. This is because it is impossible to develop

Key point

Definition:
The term
emic comes from
phonemic, or the
meaning of sounds;
emic approaches
seek to understand
the meaning of
people's lives,
as they themselves
define them

**Cross
Reference:**
See Book 3,
Chapter 3, on
elicitation methods
designed to discover
how people think

the rapport necessary for good ethnographic under-standing and data collection if social distance is maintained between researchers and informants. *A hallmark of anthro-pology as a discipline always has been its dedication to understanding the perspective of the people living in the communities under study;* the search for such "local mean-ings" is called an **emic approach.** Accurate recording of local meanings and understandings requires intensive observa-tions and in-depth interviews (see Bernard, 1995; Le-Compte & Preissle, 1993; Pelto & Pelto, 1978); specific subfields of the social sciences, including cognitive anthro-pology and sociological studies of the social construction of reality, are especially committed to the development of methods that assess how people think and believe (Weller & Romney, 1988; Werner & Schoepfle, 1987a, 1987b). For ethnographers, working to create such understanding and rapport can produce dilemmas, especially when the ethnog-raphers are trying to understand and develop empathy for practices and beliefs that are foreign to or even antithetical to their own. Anthropologists have long coped with these kinds of conflicts by adhering to a position of *cultural relativism,* which permits them to argue that although the practices and beliefs may not be shared by, or even valid for, the ethnographer, they can be legitimately studied and understood as shared by and valid for the people under study. Thus, although they may not be neutral at all regard-ing the practices *outside of the field site,* within the field site, and while analyzing and presenting data, the ethnographer is constrained by principles that forbid criticizing what the informants do or believe on the basis of ethnographers' perspectives or values.

The stance of neutrality often has been interpreted as mandating that researchers must never intervene in or try to change the lives of the people they study. However, many applied ethnographers conduct and study interventions, or are hired specifically because study populations desire change and feel that research results can help bring this about. Furthermore, critical theorists and some feminists argue that unless the research helps the people under study more fully understand the conditions in which they live and even, perhaps, improve them, it has no validity (Lather, 1986). Similarly, all feminists argue that the particular life experiences of women and the way these experiences differ sufficiently from those of men to mandate an approach to research that is cognizant of both the researcher's "standpoint" (Hartsock, 1983) and the impact that the research will have on the people studied. Critical theorists argue that one's standpoint derives from one's relative position of economic and social privilege within the social structure of a society; it is affected also by the relative advantage or disadvantage one enjoys, given one's race, gender, regional origins, religious affiliation, gender orientation, or a wide range of other factors that are used to discriminate among groups in a society. Feminists and action researchers alike (see Schensul & Schensul, 1978) argue that standpoints affect both the kinds of questions researchers find interesting and the interpretations they apply to data once the data are collected. These researchers mandate a careful analysis of one's standpoint and the blind spots or biases that it creates not only before research begins, but throughout one's career as an investigator. Specific value orientations underpin the theoretical paradigms that we have outlined in Book 1; researchers generally will select a paradigm that matches both the field situation and the ethnographer's own values.

Finally, feminist and critical researchers argue that it is dishonest and unethical not to make clear to research participants what one's background and ideological commitments are (Roman, 1992, 1993). Thus, contemporary applied ethnography tends to advocate an "in the trenches" stance regarding interaction with research participants. Thus, in this volume, we have addressed these issues, locat-

Cross Reference: See Book 1 for a more extensive discussion of critical and postmodern theories and paradigms used to inform social science researchers

ing the ethnographic researcher and his or her team of collaborators squarely in the context of their work: as identifiers and solvers of problems in communities and organizations inhabited by diverse and sometimes contentious human beings.

We also make clear that one of the most important attributes an ethnographer can bring to his or her project is a keen ability to engage in *self-reflection*. Without self-reflection, ethnographers are unlikely to be able to take stock of how they are perceived by others in the field. As a consequence, they are unlikely to be cognizant of potential gaps, errors, or biases in the data they collect because of how research participants felt about them and censored their discussions accordingly. The unreflective ethnographer—a term that is nearly oxymoronic unless applied to someone who does poor ethnography—also is not able to learn from the inevitable mistakes made in the field or to identify potential misunderstandings or dangerous situations before they become very serious, or even, in rare cases, life threatening. At the end of Chapter 1, we describe strategies that ethnographers use to enhance their powers of self-reflection.

Creating a Field Identity

In the early days of ethnographic research, researchers usually were foreigners or strangers to the study site—at least in the initial stages of investigation. Experienced ethnographers were quite aware that no community would tolerate for very long a stranger who did not seem to have any purpose for being present and who asked all kinds of questions. Thus, one of the first tasks that novice ethnographers were urged to accomplish was the construction of a field identity or **cover story**. Early ethnographers often simply arrived at their research sites, unknown to anyone in the community. They had to find a way to explain why they

Definition: A cover story provides an introductory position or initial identity for a researcher new to the research site

were there with a story that served to legitimate their presence by providing them with an introductory role or social identity. Without such an identity, members of the community would define them as irrelevant, nonpeople, ghosts, or worse—as spies, saboteurs, witches, or people who might do harm to others. For this reason, ethnographers often presented an initial identity on which they had decided before they arrived at the research site. The cover story that they used to present such an identity usually was a simplified, nontechnical, but accurate portrayal of who the researcher was and what he or she planned to do. In the pages that follow, we define both cover stories and the special kinds of identities that ethnographers need when working in applied or collaborative settings. We also make a clear distinction between field identities and accompanying cover stories, and "undercover" stories, which we feel are unethical.

➤•➤•➤ **EXAMPLE 1.2**

CREATING A FIELD IDENTITY IN SHORT GRASS

The problem was to gain access to behavior settings in which Short Grass [Canada] Indians would communicate things about themselves that were not ordinarily accessible to Whites. I had to be defined as a "safe" person, one who could be trusted not to shatter the delicate balance of Indian-White relationships, and before whom the usual presentation of Indian self-image to White could be dropped. . . . The immediate suspicion that I was a spy from the Indian Affairs Branch was dispelled when it became clear that I was not a Canadian citizen.[2] . . . When it became apparent that my car was as liable to be stopped and searched by Mounties [police] as were those of Indians, the possibility that I was an agent of the government was similarly discounted . . . [as were suspicions] that I was a spy for American oil companies . . . a communist spy . . . a White man in search of the sexual favors of [Indian] women . . . [or] an American draft dodger. (Braroe, 1975, pp. 20-21)

➤•➤•➤

> ### Rules of Thumb for Construction of Cover Stories
>
> Cover stories should simply serve as an introduction or initial identity for the ethnographer. Therefore, they should:
>
> — Not be too specific lest they limit the researchers' options for role taking or the information that community members offer
>
> — Be safe; that is, they should not present the researcher as someone with whom association could be risky
>
> — Be true stories, although they do not have to tell all the details about a researcher's role because local people often do not understand the technicalities of researchers' work
>
> — Try to avoid partisan affiliation or being identified with one or another faction in the community.
>
> — Avoid close identification with anyone known to be an authority figure or person with special interests or biases.
>
> — Be created with knowledge of the community in mind.
>
> — Be directly connected with the research to be done, so that they will reflect what people actually see the ethnographer doing, and people will know what the researcher is looking for.

EXAMPLE 1.3 ◆━●━◆━●━◆

CREATING A FIELD IDENTITY THAT USES PEOPLE'S
PARTIAL UNDERSTANDINGS ABOUT RESEARCHERS

Rosalie Wax was the first social scientist to study life in the internment camps to which Japanese residents of the United States were confined during World War II. Initially, she found it impossible to do (or to explain to residents) the participant observation her project required, given the suspicion that the Japanese residents had of anybody they thought might be associated with the camps' officials. Deciding that it was her job to convince the camp residents that she was the kind of person they could trust, Wax began to behave more like a formal interviewer than a participant and observer.

I undertook studies that had little connection with the kind of data I was supposed to be getting. I invented questionnaires and interviewed women on how they thought evacuation had altered their way of life. I interviewed parents on what they thought evacuation had done to their children. I interviewed anyone at all for information and attitudes on social stratification in Japan and the United States. I talked to [community leaders about] what they thought about juvenile delinquency. (Wax, 1971, pp. 75-76)

Residents were familiar with this more formal kind of research; Wax got to know people by doing these studies, and they "gave respondents a reasonable story to tell to curious neighbors" who might have wondered why camp members were talking with her. They also helped to clarify what Wax's ultimate role was to be: to observe and ask questions.

━•━•━ **EXAMPLE 1.4**

WHEN PARTICIPANTS MISUNDERSTAND THE RESEARCHER'S TOPIC AND ACT ABNORMALLY BECAUSE THE COVER STORY IS NOT RELATED TO THE RESEARCH QUESTION

A teacher participating in LeCompte's study of fourth-grade classrooms told her students that the researcher was observing their class in order to "write a book" about life in fourth grade. The students decided to give LeCompte better material to write about by clowning around, wisecracking in response to teacher questions, and generally making instruction impossible and life miserable for the teacher. In response to the teacher's pleas to help her get the students to settle down, LeCompte had to redefine her role as "author" (and the students' roles as "actors") by explaining that her book was about everyday and *serious* work in classrooms.

━•━•━

LeCompte's cover story fulfilled some of the criteria listed above; it *was* simple, true, and safe. However, it thoroughly confused the children because it was not linked clearly enough to the real task that LeCompte was trying to accomplish.

It is equally important for cover stories to avoid creating preconceptions about how people in the community

should act toward the ethnographer. Thus, although it may
seem quite tempting to enter a community as the "adopted"
member of a respected family or under the sponsorship of
authority figures, doing so can be risky. For example, if the
ethnographer is identified with a high-status family, lower-
status people in the community may find it difficult to
approach him/her. Similarly, if the ethnographer is identified with authority figures such as social workers, administrators, evaluators, government agents, or someone from a
specific community interest group or constituency, people
with whom the researcher may wish to have candid interactions are likely to censor what they say and do in accordance with their customary behavior vis-à-vis such individuals. Sometimes, these identities are unavoidable because
some kind of sponsorship or allegiance usually is necessary
before a researcher can even get in the door. Therefore,
ethnographers should simply try to create a plausible entry
story and expand upon its details as interaction ensues in
the field. Most important is for researchers to realize that
any form of identification that leads research participants
to act differently from their ordinary demeanor (as in Example 1.4 above) or conform to what they think the researcher expects or wants is problematic.

We must add that adhering to all of these suggestions
requires more knowledge of the community than ethnographers usually have in the initial fieldwork stages. Thus, it
is useful for the ethnographer to first learn something about
the community that he or she plans to enter by talking to
former residents, teachers, public figures, politicians, or
relatives of residents to find out how people "line up" and
how to avoid—to the extent possible—becoming affiliated
too early with various contentious groups.

JUGGLING FIELDWORK REQUIREMENTS WITH
REQUIREMENTS OF ROLES ACQUIRED IN THE FIELD SITE

A Senegalese male medical anthropologist was working in two urban areas of Senegal. Both areas included members of two groups important to his study: the Dimba, a traditional self-help society of women and men who engage in reproductive health education, and the Laobe, an ethnic group in which women traders sell reproductive health goods. He was told that he could learn more about the Dimba if he agreed to be inducted formally into the society as an assistant to the Dimba "father," a senior male counselor. In that role, he was able to do the ethnographic work necessary to introduce an AIDS prevention program. However, at the same time, in his role as an assistant to a senior counselor, he was regularly "on call" for consultation on problems men encountered with reproductive health and fatherhood—even from his birth city 300 miles away. He had to do both counseling and fieldwork, while at the same time considering the degree to which his counselor role influenced behavior of his research subjects in the field.

━●━●━●

Ethnographers often enter communities with a specific research assignment or problem to solve. In such cases, the problem itself determines some of the associations they must make. Ethnographers interested in health care problems may find themselves of necessity seeking the help of highly educated health care professionals who may or may not be perceived positively by the community. The same health care professionals may, in turn, believe community recipients of health services to be unreliable or poor informants. In such cases, ethnographers will need to make it clear to all constituents that their responsibility is to respond to and record the viewpoints of all community members.

Special Considerations for
Collaborative and Applied Projects

The need to create initial field identities is less problematic
for applied ethnographers, in large part because of the way
that such ethnographers become involved with communities. Generally, they are not strangers, at least to the organizational administrators or community leaders involved. In
addition, although they still begin research with rather
open-ended exploration (i.e., with a search for an answer to
the question, "What's going on here?"), they do come for
specific purposes—to study a problem or phenomenon that
already has been identified as in need of investigation—and
they are known (and expected) to possess the skills and
expertise needed to carry out such a study. Thus, their
identities are quite clear from the outset, though they must
be presented in a culturally appropriate way, as the following example illustrates.

EXAMPLE 1.6   ➤●➤●➤

CONDUCTING RESEARCH ON COMMUNITY UNDERSTANDING OF ALZHEIMER'S DISEASE

The Institute for Community Research (ICR) joined forces with several other institutions to conduct a formative study of community knowledge of Alzheimer's disease
(AD), and to assess ways of disseminating information about it in the Puerto Rican
community. Members of the research staff decided to interview families, service
providers, and community institutions—botanicas selling herbs and religious icons,
pharmacies, and community-based organizations—to identify differences in the
meaning of Alzheimer's disease, and potential distribution channels for accurate
information on diagnosis and management of the disease.

ICR researchers discussed the project and determined that they could identify
themselves as researching perspectives on AD to service providers and community
institutions, but not to families. The researchers felt that families would be upset if
researchers used the term Alzheimer's disease because it was associated with loss of

control and mental health problems, both of which family members feared. This might result in their reluctance to participate in the study. Thus, the researchers decided to identify themselves to families as people investigating health problems associated with aging. They planned to ask about symptom identification first, and only later about dementias—including Alzheimer's disease.

➤•➤•➤

Despite these precautions, the issue of affiliation with a particular constituency, the wrong constituency, or with multiple constituencies is relevant; roles that ethnographers necessarily adopt and that become ascribed to them do affect how they will act in the field, the kind of data to which they will have access, how they will interact with people inside and outside of the study site, and the kinds of duties and responsibilities they will be defined as having.

Often, people in the field do not understand just what a collaborative relationship with an applied ethnographer means. They can confuse ethnographic work with the traditional stereotype of researchers that we discussed earlier in this chapter. Initially, they may not view the researcher as a partner, and they also may be reluctant to ask for help or reveal that they have problems. Applied ethnographers generally will need to construct three kinds of field identities:

1. In relation to staff of the organizations or members of the community who invited them to do a study
2. In relation to the people and situations about and with whom information is sought
3. In relation to the scientific community that may have funded them and that would benefit from the results of their work

These three categories sometimes, but not always, overlap, as we discuss in the second chapter of this book. As the **Ethnographer's Toolkit** makes clear, ethnography does require very complex and multilayered sets of relationships!

Going Undercover

Cover stories should not be confused with going undercover. The construction of undercover stories, as we indicated earlier, we believe to be unethical. In most cases, these stories will not survive scrutiny by review panels whose task is to ensure that people are not deceived or tricked into being research participants. *Whereas cover stories provide an initial identity, undercover stories are intended to deceive, as, for example, when researchers pretend to be drug users in order to study addicts, or homosexuals in order to study the behavior of that population* (Bolton, 1995). Undercover identities also can involve simply not identifying oneself as a researcher in order to study stigmatized or illegal behavior, as Humphries (1970a, 1970b) did when he observed and recorded homosexual behavior in public toilets. Some methodologists *do* advocate the adoption of false identities, especially in cases where the behavior of interest is secret or illegal, or where letting community members know that one is a researcher would preclude access to the site. Studies of drug distributors, cult members, gangs, or revolutionary and secret societies fall into these categories. *However, we do not advocate going undercover for several reasons.* First, it is difficult to maintain a false identity among the intimate relationships and long periods of residence in the field that are customarily required in ethnography. Getting caught is always a danger, and being unmasked can both destroy the trust between researcher and informants upon which good ethnographic data collection is predicated and endanger the ethnographer. Second, most institutional review boards (IRBs) forbid the use of undercover stories because they make it difficult for people to give truly informed consent to their participation. Third, because they are designed to deceive, undercover stories can be unethical. Finally, the very nature of collaborative and applied ethnography described in the **Ethnographer's**

Key point

Key point

Definition: Institutional review boards are committees mandated by the U.S. government that oversee the ethical treatment of human subjects in research

Toolkit precludes working undercover, because the process of problem solving requires collaboration with and full disclosure to most, if not all, participants in the community.

Being a Learner

Regardless of the content of an ethnographer's cover story, the most appropriate role for ethnographers to establish with anyone in the research site is that of a helpful learner. With staff members from institutional partners, that role can be enhanced if the researcher is perceived to be a good collaborator, colleague, and coresearcher. With people in the population under study, the wisest choice for ethnographers is the role or identity of a learner or student. Such a stance permits the ethnographer to practice a kind of naïveté about the practices and beliefs of the study population, and it also legitimates why the ethnographer might be engaging in so much observation or asking so many questions. *Ethnographers must be learners, and as such, they* **Key point** *must position themselves so that people in the community feel comfortable teaching them.* To be viewed as "in need of being taught," ethnographers find ways to engage legitimately in the primary strategies humans use for learning: watching, listening to, and asking questions of people who are practiced in what is to be learned. The anthropologist Jacquetta Burnett (1974) advised novice ethnographers to learn about a community the way children learn: with careful observation, endless curiosity, lots of questions, and an open mind. Whereas ethnographers clearly are not children and should avoid resembling ignoramuses or dolts, they also should avoid seeming to know too much about the topic about which they are asking questions. "Know-it-alls" cannot learn and certainly are not in need of being taught!

A well-known anthropologist, James Spradley (1979), argued that ethnographers who already seem quite familiar with the life, activities, beliefs, or tasks of the community under study will not be told much by informants, because informants do not want to embarrass themselves by telling ethnographers something they already know. However, Spradley also notes that it is particularly difficult to maintain such a stance in cases where ethnographers are, in fact, studying what they already know. Such cases are fairly typical for applied ethnographers, who can be called upon to study the institutions or programs for which they work, or in which they have previous, similar experience. It is quite easy to forget to ask detailed questions about or take copious notes on activities whose routines or history one already knows. Doing so, however, ignores the fact that what one person does routinely may be done, explained, or conceptualized differently by others or in other organizations.

EXAMPLE 1.7   ━•━•━

HOW BEING PERCEIVED AS SOMEONE "IN THE KNOW" IMPEDES DATA COLLECTION

A graduate student in a university's business school was interested in studying innovative software uses among several telecommunications companies. He began by interviewing the directors of research and development for each of the companies but found that it was difficult to get them to spell out in detail the different stages in their product development and training programs. "I don't need to tell you about *this!*" was a common statement made by the interviewees; "You've been studying this in your classes for years!" In fact, the student found that the practice of most companies differed considerably from the practices taught in the business school; they differed considerably among themselves as well. The novice researcher had to develop techniques that reassured interviewees that although he had, in fact, studied *something* about such practices, he really was interested in the particular way *they* defined problems or carried out their work.

━•━•━

Leaving out important bits of description because researchers and informants both know that each knows about the issues under consideration also does not take into account that people who read the reports of a study or who use the data may have considerably less shared knowledge of such practices, beliefs, or history than the original informants and ethnographers. Failure to document fully all aspects of the research site and population may result in significant and dangerous gaps in the investigative record. By the same token, hearing the same or only slightly different story again and again gives the ethnographer confidence that he or she has actually collected an authentic, or valid, story, complete with all of its nuances of difference. Thus, the ethnographer's task in any situation is to reassure informants continually that researchers really *are* learners, interested in minute details of history, behavior, and belief, and that they really have *not* already heard what is being recounted.

Being perceived as a learner or student is not always easy, nor are the realities of how applied ethnographers are perceived and what they are called upon to do in the field. It is especially difficult when significant status differentials exist between researcher and informants.

◆—•—◆—•—◆   **EXAMPLE 1.8**

BRIDGING CLASS DIFFERENCES IN THE FIELD

Ethnographic field researcher Nitza Diaz is a young, middle-class Puerto Rican woman from a family of educators and activists, who is trained as an ethnographer. She was involved in a study designed to collect data on Puerto Rican children's activity expenditures. Part of her work required her to visit the homes of more than 70 children at least twice. The first time involved describing to mothers the study and record-keeping requirements; the second visit involved an in-depth, semistructured interview on perceptions of chronic health problems (cardiovascular disease, cancer, diabetes, and arthritis) and steps that could be taken to prevent these diseases. She was able to obtain access to caregivers and to establish excellent field relationships. The refusal rate for the study was very low. She was very successful at convincing caregivers and children to record data on energy outputs measured with caltracs, or electronic instruments for measuring energy unit and caloric outputs. But when she questioned her respondents about the etiology, prevention, and management of chronic health problems, they argued that she should know the answers already because she was more educated than they. Recognizing the class difference between themselves and Diaz—evidenced by educational disparities—the respondents felt uncomfortable telling her how to care for disabilities that they felt she knew more about than they did.

Cross Reference: See Book 2, Chapter 4, and Book 5, Chapter 2, for techniques used in listening and recording fieldnotes

Regardless of obstacles created by differences between researchers and research participants in status, gender, ethnicity, or education, it is important for applied ethnographers to work toward roles or identities that permit them to be good listeners and make it possible to observe widely and record what they observe. Good listeners are good learners; good observers must be able to record their observations fully and competently. Even where researcher characteristics and ascribed roles make being a learner or a student difficult, the ethnographers' roles must facilitate these activities.

> ## *Suggestions for Being a Good Ethnographic Listener*
>
> - Learn and adopt the cultural cues that denote "attentive listening" within the cultural context of your research site.
> - Ask lots of questions.
> - Make sure that your informants talk more than you do.
> - Focus the conversation on your informant's experiences and background rather than your own.
> - Start out by counting to three—slowly—after your informant stops speaking and before you say something else, then adjust your own response time accordingly. The rate of speaking and thinking across cultures is different, sometimes slower, sometimes faster.
> - Write down what your informants say. It gives people time to think and makes them feel that what they said was important.

It is important to remember that the above suggestions will not work in every culture, because what constitutes good listening in one culture may be defined as bad manners in another. In North American and many European cultures, for example, good listeners look directly into the eyes of their fellow conversationalists while they are talking. However, among many American Indian cultures, direct stares are considered to be signs of aggression or hostility. European Americans also speak quickly, tend to interrupt each other, and begin speaking as soon as a pause in the conversation occurs; American Indians wait for a considerable period of time between a speaker's phrases to make sure that the speaker has finished talking. Norwegians signify that they are attending closely to what a speaker is saying with a sharp and audible intake of breath, accompanied by an upward jerk of the chin. By contrast, European Americans repeatedly nod their heads up and down, while saying "uh huh." Sri Lankans show agreement by shaking their heads sideways, a sign that would signal disagreement to the average European American. Learning the postures, gestures, and speech patterns that accompany polite listening in the research site will greatly facilitate an ethnographer's ability to be viewed as a good listener and learner.

In the next section, we discuss how the characteristics that ethnographers bring to the field "with their bodies" (Metz, 1978) affect their relationships in the field. We then describe the roles that ethnographers acquire by virtue of their friendships and professional relationships, the tasks they perform, the institutional affiliations they possess, and the purposes for and outcomes of their research. We also address ways to ameliorate differences in status between researchers and those whom they study and with whom they work.

COPING WITH REACTIONS IN THE FIELD: PERSONAL, PHYSICAL, AND BACKGROUND CHARACTERISTICS OF THE RESEARCHER

This section is concerned with the bodily or physical, personality, and background characteristics of the researcher. Some researchers have advocated being as unobtrusive as a "fly on the wall"; others have asserted that they wished they could be invisible when in the field doing research. Some of this desire derives from the discomfort researchers feel when interacting with people while simultaneously observing them, listening in on conversations, and recording interactions. A good part of it, however, derives from the fact that if researchers were invisible, they would not have to worry about the conclusions people might make based on their appearance or what informants might think the researchers' background meant. For example, researchers could stop worrying about what their adolescent street informants thought about (for example) a middle-aged, well-dressed, gray-haired, female researcher—and how those thoughts would censor what the adolescents were willing to talk about in the researcher's presence. Nor would the researcher need to worry about what those teenagers thought about being seen by others—especially peer group friends—while in her company.

EXAMPLE 1.9   ━●━●━●━

WHY NAVAJOS VISITED THE ETHNOGRAPHER ONLY AT NIGHT

An ethnographer studying implementation of a Navajo/English bilingual program at a school district in the Navajo Nation in the southwestern United States found that Navajo parents and community members would never visit her home during the day. She learned that although her informants trusted her as an individual, they did not want their neighbors and friends to know that they were socializing in the home of a *bilagaana*—the Navajo name for "white people." By coming and going under cover of darkness, they could visit without creating gossip within specific factions in the Navajo community.

━●━●━●━

WHY TEEN ACTION RESEARCHERS WOULD NOT TAKE
RESEARCHERS TO VISIT THEIR NEIGHBORHOOD

Investigator J. Schensul and a team of ethnographers are conducting a study of young hard drug users between the ages of 16 and 24. Incorporated into the study is the opportunity for young people who might be former or even current drug users to act as consultants to the study. Two young adult men, 19 and 20, volunteered to participate as advisors to one of the ethnographers in return for an internship stipend and class credits. Both had experienced life on the streets, and one had strong leadership skills, visibility, and a reputation for being invincible within the community. Both claimed they knew many people, and one said that everyone respected him. These young men were quite comfortable talking to the ethnographers in the offices of the Institute for Community Research, where they were participants in a summer youth research institute, or in a neutral restaurant downtown, but after several months, they were still reluctant to take researchers into their neighborhoods or introduce them to their peers, since one of them was trying to leave his street network, and the other wanted to maintain separation between his professional and "street" affiliations.

━●━●━

At the same time, experienced fieldworkers know quite well that ethnographers cannot be invisible or work only at night, and therefore, who they are in real life affects profoundly how they can behave, with whom they can interact, and how they interact in the field. We now discuss some of the most important characteristics that ethnographers bring to the field with them and how these characteristics might affect research activities. We discuss the impact of these characteristics not because we believe that researchers should try to eliminate them—an impossibility—but because we believe that before they become skilled and competent fieldworkers, ethnographers must develop an understanding of how their own personal characteristics—gender, age, physical features, clothing and style, culture, class, and educational level—are likely to affect the process and outcome of their research efforts.

Gender

One of the most obvious characteristics that researchers bring to the field with them is their gender. No culture is without its norms regarding proper gender role behavior. These constrain the places where men and women are allowed to be, with whom they are allowed to speak, the kinds of information deemed appropriate for them to have, and the kinds of activities in which they are permitted to participate.

EXAMPLE 1.11   ➡•➡•➡

SOCIAL DISTANCE BETWEEN MALE RESEARCHER
AND FEMALE RESIDENTS IN SHORT GRASS

During my first summer in Short Grass, I [a white male researcher] had insurmountable difficulties in talking with women. If there were no men home when I visited an Indian house, women would not answer my knocks at the door and pretended no one was there. In mixed company, women hardly ever contributed to the conversation and would avoid even eye contact on streets in town. (Braroe, 1975, p. 22)

➡•➡•➡

Ethnographers sometimes can transcend these constraints; male researchers can learn something of the life of women by asking men, and they often can talk to women under special circumstances or about less intimate issues. Braroe, cited above, indicates that when his wife joined him during his second summer in the Short Grass community, it became easier for him to communicate with women; some even came to tea at his house. And by the end of his several years of fieldwork, women talked to him as freely as men did, even when men were not present.

Braroe encountered social practices that made it difficult for women in general to speak to men. However, some topics are especially difficult to discuss in cross-gender groups. It is difficult, for example, for women to talk about many issues of intimate concern—for example, childbirth, nursing, sexual health practices, relationships with spouses, abuse—to a researcher who differs from them in gender and social status.

EXAMPLE 1.12

REDUCING STATUS DIFFERENCES TO IMPROVE COMMUNICATION ABOUT BEHAVIOR TOO INTIMATE TO DESCRIBE TO MALE RESEARCHERS

Male Latino physicians were unable to engage Mexican American women in conversations about their prebirth, labor, and postbirth experiences and about their own health and that of their children because of gender and status differences between the doctors and the women. However, when *female* anthropologists trained groups of community leaders to conduct in-depth interviews and surveys with the same women, they were able to elicit detailed stories about the same issues.

EXAMPLE 1.13

USING SAME-SEX RESEARCHERS TO RUN FOCUS GROUPS ON SEXUAL BEHAVIOR IN SRI LANKA

A mixed-gender research team of Americans and Sri Lankans was conducting a study of sexual behavior and sex risk in an urban area of Sri Lanka. Knowing that cross-gender discussions of sexuality are considered taboo in Sri Lanka, the team decided to hold separate interviews and focus groups for young men and women, with young female ethnographers collecting data on early and current experiences with partners from the same and opposite sex from young women, and young male ethnographers collecting similar data from young men. The interviews, which went very well, also entailed collection of detailed data on 23 explicit sexual behaviors. Respondents were eager to talk with their same-sex interviewers about their concerns and about issues of reproductive health. Then, once both groups—and the interviewers themselves—were prepared for cross-gender discussions, it became possible to hold a successful mixed-gender focus group to discuss ways of negotiating sexual decision making in social situations (Nastasi et al., 1998).

Sexual mores also exacerbate cross-gender relationships. In most societies, women also are viewed by men as potential sexual objects, regardless of their status. This factor complicates the lives of fieldworkers, because the attentive listening and the studied—and scholarly—interest in informants' lives and stories that are the stock in trade of the competent ethnographer can be interpreted by informants to be *personal* interest and an invitation to intimacy. It is made doubly difficult because interviewing often requires taking an informant aside and interviewing him or her in a quiet place, often isolated from other people—a kind of intimacy that can be misinterpreted, at best, and tabooed, at worst, in many cultures.

EXAMPLE 1.14   ━•━•━

CONFUSING ATTENTIVE ETHNOGRAPHIC LISTENING WITH SEXUAL INTEREST

A young female ethnographer, a novice member of an evaluation team, attended a 3-day retreat for researchers, teachers, community members, and administrators involved in a community-based school restructuring project. Part of her job was to conduct ongoing interviews with teachers in the project to assess their understanding of and commitment to the project. At the end of the second day of meetings, one of her informants, a young male social studies teacher, told her he had time to finish their interview and invited her to his room, where it was quiet enough for her to tape-record his remarks. After setting up her recorder, the ethnographer was dismayed to find her informant taking off his coat and shirt, telling her that it was time to go beyond all the "nice talk" in which they had been engaged and "get serious."

━•━•━

Situations such as the one above can be avoided if fieldworkers take care never to become so isolated from other people that extrication from awkward or dangerous situations is impossible. It is also very important for women working alone in the field to learn from key informants and others familiar with the sexual norms of the culture the specific cues that attract sexual attention. For women in most cultures, these include living alone, having male friends from home visit alone, wearing low-cut blouses or short skirts, or walking alone after a specific time in the evening. It is good practice for women to avoid such behaviors. Men also must learn the cues that make them sexual targets, such as talking with a woman alone in a private spot.

In general, we believe that sex and fieldwork do not mix very well, even though some methodologists argue that because ethnographers are human beings, they are subject to the same romantic and human inclinations in the field as out of it (see Bernard, 1995). Notwithstanding, we believe that even without romantic attachments, it is difficult enough to manage the ambiguities of friendship with the key informants and colleagues upon whom ethnographers depend in the field; these special kinds of friendship do, after all, have as their initial and fundamental basis the ethnographer's need to elicit information, rather than the bases upon which ordinary friendships are founded. That "need to know" often strains relationships under normal conditions of acquaintanceship. When friends and colleagues who are informants also become lovers, additional strains are created. Furthermore, stresses in or the breakup of a romantic relationship can seriously jeopardize access to crucial information. In Example 1.14, the ethnographer was trying to do a good job and believed that her informant would talk more freely in private. She ended up unable to complete the interview and in a compromising situation.

In general, we believe that few pieces of data are so valuable that they warrant ethnographers risking their physical, emotional, or mental health; their well-being; or their lives. Using same-sex interviewers or teams of interviewers can alleviate sexual mishaps to some degree, but this is not always possible. A more secure safeguard is the savvy and vigilance of an experienced fieldworker; this should be supported by a vigilant project director lest entire research programs be jeopardized by the behavior of a team member.

EXAMPLE 1.15   ◄══•◄══•◄══

HOW A TEAM MEMBER'S ROMANCE DESTROYED A RESEARCH PROJECT

A professor of education and his team of graduate students had been studying the process of innovation in an alternative school. The members of the research team were viewed by the administration as having the same status as teachers or administrators—and certainly higher than student teacher interns. One of the female graduate students previously had taught classes in the School of Education; there she met and began to date an undergraduate student who was doing his student teaching internship at the school. The couple often was seen together around the school premises. Because the school district had strong policies forbidding intimate relationships between subordinates and superiors, and because the relationship between the research team member and the student intern was viewed as flagrant, the professor was told to leave the school and to close down his 2-year-long study.

◄══•◄══•◄══

In a contrasting case, a novice female researcher in another project avoided potential difficulty when she was asked for a date by a young male teacher by first contacting the project director to learn what school district and project policies governed such situations.

Age

Age is another characteristic that, like gender, is impossible to alter and affects the kinds of people and information to which ethnographers have access. Depending upon the population of interest, the ethnographer's age may either facilitate or impede data collection. Age also influences the kinds of people who will feel comfortable associating with the researcher. Some female anthropologists have argued that older women have fewer difficulties in the field. Intimacies in the field cease to be problematic because older women are less often seen as sex objects. In many cultures, older people are granted a status and respect that younger researchers cannot enjoy. On the other hand, closeness in age—or the appearance of closeness—between research participants and ethnographers sometimes can be helpful. Donna Deyhle (1986) was able to win the confidence of the Native American students she wished to study because, as a young woman who herself possessed a pair of the parachute pants that all the young people coveted, she could talk with them about common interests in clothing, hang out around the school as a student might without being too noticeably adult, and actually participate in adolescent break-dancing activities. Similarly, in her study of teenage punks, Leslie Roman (1988) was able to "go native" to some degree because she appeared to be about the age of the punks and, when attending rock concerts, she could dress in the kinds of clothing they favored. *It should be kept in mind that in some cases, it is impossible for the ethnographer to blend in, and different strategies for building rapport must be developed.* Had Deyhle and Roman not looked so young, they could have hired as research assistants "junior ethnographers" (Heath, 1996) or other individuals who were closer in age to the teenagers in the study and who could, therefore, interact more easily and communicate more freely with them. Shirley Brice Heath's use of junior ethnographers to study adolescent artists resembles the concept of the ethnographic team—a group of researchers that vary in gender, age, ethnicity, and level of training. Team research permits ethnographic research to be much more unobtrusive, as members go about in pairs, or as researchers are selected, insofar as is possible, to match with the respondents or informants from whom they seek information. The work of ethnographic teams is not limited to gaining access to

Key point

research sites and collecting data, however; in the second chapter of this book, we discuss how ethnographic teams participate in a collective process of analysis and interpretation of data, the result of which is a socially constructed portrait of the phenomenon under study.

Although trying to blend in or to use surrogate researchers is effective in some situations, it is impossible in others. In most societies, certain information is not deemed appropriate for young people to possess, as Margaret Mead (1928) later discovered in her study of young Samoan girls. As a young woman herself, she simply was not told of many things about which Samoan elders thought she was too young to know. Gender and age often create conflated problems; young females may be privy to information available to women but not to men of any age. Although young male and female ethnographers are more likely to have social problems with informants of the opposite sex, age alone does not preclude ethnographers from being considered attractive social or sexual partners by members of the participant community. In fact, although in many societies, older women cease to be viewed as sexual objects, they still may be sought out as counselors to younger people who seek access to various forms of cultural knowledge or initiation into specific social or sexual behaviors (Silva et al., 1997).

Physical Features

Characteristics such as body size, hair and skin color, and facial features cause informants and research participants to make judgments about an ethnographer's competence, attractiveness, and energy levels. These judgments, in turn, determine what informants are willing to divulge and the extent to which they will interact with ethnographers—at least in the initial stages of research. Judgments are context specific, so it is necessary to determine the possible influence of appearance in each cultural setting that the ethnographer enters. Furthermore, judgments may influence initial reactions to the researcher, causing the ethnographer to work harder to gain acceptance. We believe that with perseverance and good intentions, such prejudices eventually can be overcome, and researchers will come to be perceived as "real people," friends and associates in the field setting.

At the risk of seeming to stereotype, we list a few such characteristics and how they affect perception in western European society; perceptions may be quite different in other cultures.

Prejudices Linked to Personal Appearance in Western Cultures

- Obesity is a sign of laziness and lack of intelligence.
- Slim people are attractive, energetic, and intelligent.
- Very thin people—especially if they are females—are likely to be wealthy.
- Tall people have leadership qualities; however, extremely tall people are clumsy and unathletic.
- Short people are aggressive.
- A soft voice denotes weakness or indecisiveness.
- People who are very beautiful or handsome are not extremely intelligent or competent. (The common stereotype of the "beautiful dumb blonde" applies to both men and women.)
- People who wear glasses are intelligent.
- People with red hair lose their tempers easily.
- Good athletes (especially those in football) are poor students.
- Very good students, especially if they are girls, are not attractive or athletic.

EXAMPLE 1.16   ━●━●━●

EQUATING PHYSICAL CHARACTERISTICS WITH
MORAL CHARACTERISTICS OR COMPETENCE

A project director received a number of complaints about one member of her research team—a man who was extremely overweight. Despite the man's extensive prior research experience, his excellence in all other assignments, and the confidence expressed in him by the project director, her counterparts in the community organization continued to argue that her assistant could not carry out his assigned tasks. "There must be something wrong with him. Why doesn't he take better care of himself? Can't he go on a diet?" they asked. Preoccupied by their association of great weight with an undesirable personality or incompetence, and not wanting to interact with the staff member, the community organization staff never invited the assistant to informal gatherings at which much project business was transacted. Not until the man left the project for another job and the project director was able to assign another assistant—one who was less experienced but who was thin and attractive—did the complaints cease and more fruitful interaction between staff and researcher begin.

━●━●━

Standards of attractiveness or physical acceptability vary by culture, however. A contrasting list of common stereotypical assumptions about physical features from Sri Lanka might look quite different:

- Thin people are poor and uneducated.
- Men who wear the national dress (white shirt and sarong) on the street are rural farmers; professionals do not wear a sarong in public.
- Women who wear slacks are upper class, have traveled internationally, and are likely to be somewhat arrogant.

WHERE IS FAT ATTRACTIVE? DIFFERENCES IN BEAUTY BETWEEN THE UNITED STATES AND SOMALIA

LeCompte, who, at 5 feet, 6 inches, weighed more than 160 pounds by the end of her Peace Corps service, was thought to be considerably overweight by the U.S. doctor who cared for volunteers. The Somali teachers with whom she worked, however, kept urging her to eat more heartily. "Don't they pay you enough to eat?" they asked. By Somali standards, LeCompte was underfed and could not possibly have the energy needed both to teach the children in her charge and provide adult classes in the evenings. Her thin ankles (a lingering source of pride for LeCompte) were a particular source of concern to her Somali women friends, because Somali men considered thick female ankles to be a sign of attractiveness.

◆•◆•◆

Physical characteristics associated with ethnicity—such as skin color—are special cases. Some survey research methodologists advocate matching the ethnicity of interviewers with the ethnicity of potential interviewees, on the grounds that people will feel more comfortable talking with someone who resembles them. *There is some evidence to substantiate that matching interviewers and interviewees improves data quality.* Furthermore, some communities may be openly hostile to researchers whose ethnicity is different from their own.

Key point

PROTECTING A FIELDWORKER FROM RACISM

The project director for a team of educational researchers decided not to send a highly skilled African American fieldworker to collect data in a rural community in the southern United States because the school district administrators, teachers, and most of the children were white, and historical patterns of racism and discrimination in the area almost guaranteed that the fieldworker would encounter a lack of cooperation. The project director, a white woman, did the fieldwork herself and dispatched her assistant to a community in the Northwest, where racial prejudice was not so prevalent.

◆•◆•◆

On the other hand, confidential or intimate behavior may be more readily revealed to interviewers perceived to be sympathetic outsiders.

EXAMPLE 1.19   ━•━•━•━

INTERVIEWING YOUNG WOMEN IN MAURITIUS:
WHETHER OR NOT TO MATCH INTERVIEWERS TO RESPONDENTS

In 1992 and 1993, a joint American-Mauritius ethnographic research team was conducting a study of AIDS risk among young, unmarried women in the workforce. Mauritius is culturally and linguistically diverse. The major ethnic/linguistic groups are Christian Creoles (people of French and African origin), Hindu Indo-Mauritians and Indo-Mauritian Muslims originally from India, and Chinese people from southern China. All groups speak Creole, Mauritius's lingua franca, and most groups speak some French and a third language (Hindi, Urdu, Cantonese, etc.), depending on their country of origin.

Approximately 90 young women in the industrial sector were interviewed about their family and work background, their relationships with their peers, their sexual experience, and their knowledge of HIV/AIDS and sexually transmitted diseases. Interview topics were considered to be sensitive, especially because Mauritian families still place high value on female virginity and the multiethnic interview team consisted of both males and females ranging in age from 26 to 52, and because part of the interview focused on participants' sexual behaviors, partners, conflicts, and problems.

Team members and project directors gave considerable thought to what the match between interviewers and respondents should be. For the most part, interviewers and respondents were matched first by gender and language, and second by ethnicity. In some cases, foreigners—the project's lead researchers—interviewed female workers as well as managers. Foreign interviewers seemed able to elicit extensive responses despite occasional language and clear cultural differences. Occasionally, young women asked the non-Mauritian interviewers questions about their physiology, pregnancy, menstruation, and other reproductive health issues that they might not have asked a Mauritian interviewer. One of the field team members was a young American male who, despite his gender, had good results when interviewing young, unmarried women about their sexual status, including virginity. Team members concluded that foreign males as well as females could, in fact, successfully carry out interviews too sensitive for national interviewers of the same sex to conduct.

━•━•━•━

Because insiders may be viewed as already knowledgeable, it may be difficult for an interviewer who is from the same group or background as the informants to obtain detailed information that the informant feels the ethnographer already knows (see Example 1.7). Furthermore, informants may be unwilling to divulge sensitive information to an insider who might identify which members of the community have revealed community secrets.

➤•➤•➤ EXAMPLE 1.20

ALTERING DATA COLLECTION STRATEGIES IN A YOUTH-LED
PARTICIPATORY ACTION RESEARCH PROJECT
TO BETTER ELICIT SENSITIVE INFORMATION

Each summer, youth in the National Teen Action Research Center of the Institute for Community Research conduct a team research project of their choice. Two of the topics chosen in 1998 by the summer research team of 30 youth were "sex at an early age" and "factors accounting for dropping out of school." During a 6-week period, youth learned basic ethnographic field research methods, two of which involved in-depth interviewing and ethnographic surveying. As they learned each method, they had the opportunity to apply it to the collection of data related to their topic. In both groups, youth were reluctant to interview their peers in face-to-face interviews on the topics chosen for 1998 because they feared that their peers would not share accurate information about their own behavior in these areas with them. Consequently, they conducted their face-to-face, in-depth interviews with adults and used an anonymous survey with their peers.

Cross Reference: See Book 2, Chapter 8, for the definition and description of the concept of the ethnographic survey

➤•➤•➤

Patterns of deference, prejudice, and discrimination affect the access that researchers from subordinated groups within a society have to certain kinds of data. The reverse also can be true, when researchers perceived to be from privileged cultural or ethnic backgrounds are discouraged or even prevented from accessing important information about subordinated or minority populations. The U.S. Bureau of the Census, for example, often has been prevented from enumerating specific groups in the population—or from defining them in specific ways—because such groups argue that doing so either underrepresents their numbers or could single them out for racial discrimination.

In some societies, rigid formal and informal social practices can make contact between researchers and community members difficult.

EXAMPLE 1.21   ➤•➤•➤

RACE AS AN IMPEDIMENT TO RESEARCHER ACCESS

Hortense Powdermaker (1966), a white female anthropologist, found that racist patterns of social distance and avoidance made it difficult for her to carry out observations or interviews in the African American neighborhoods of the small southern community she studied in the United States in the 1940s. Blacks came to the white residences only as servants or laborers. White men were not supposed to be in the African American community unless they were collecting bills, arresting inhabitants, or on other business. A white woman had no legitimate reason for visiting blacks at all. In fact, doing so risked endangering any black male individual whom she encountered—because he might be accused of molesting or even raping her if anything went awry.

➤•➤•➤

⬥•⬥•⬥ **EXAMPLE 1.22**

HOW ETHNIC PREJUDICE CREATES SOCIAL DISTANCE

Getting to her research site on the Navajo Nation required that LeCompte fly in to the nearest airport, rent a car, and then drive for 3 hours across an isolated rural landscape. On her first trip to the "Pinnacle" community, LeCompte's flight arrived late, necessitating a 3-hour drive on a cold, dark, winter night. Stopping at a small restaurant near the airport, LeCompte asked for coffee and directions to make sure that she was on the correct road. "Whatever are you going *there* for, little lady?" asked the waiter. "All you're going to find is a bunch of drunken Indians." When she persisted in asking for directions, the waiter threw a map at her, poured her coffee, and left without charging her. "You're going to need that coffee to survive, lady, if you insist on driving to *that* place!" he retorted over his shoulder.

⬥•⬥•⬥

Cosmetics, Clothing, and Bodily Decoration: The Researcher's Visual Identity

Human beings never go naked into any social situation. Even in societies where little actual clothing is used, various forms of decoration, body or face paint, jewelry, and regalia are put on to enhance beauty, establish one's status, or maintain norms of propriety. In addition to physical props, people adopt styles of speaking, moving, and interacting with others that conform to established ideas about behavior appropriate for the kind of people they are and that establish or reinforce their identity and position within the limits of social and cultural expectations. The well-known sociologist Erving Goffman (1961) called the adornments, props, trappings, and styles of behavior that people use to establish or reinforce who they are an "identity kit." *Ethnographers need to be aware of those aspects of their customary identity kit that might offend people in the field or that might lead them to make assumptions detrimental to the relationships that ethnographers need to establish in the*

Key point

field. The anthropologist Shirley Heath (1996, personal communication), whose current work is with low-income and minority urban adolescents, asserts that she tries to be as neutral in her appearance as possible; she does not wear jewelry or clothes that make a statement, and she even limits the color of the clothing she wears to white, beige, black, and gray. She feels that doing so avoids to some extent the assumptions that people make about who you are based on what you look like; it interferes less with the natural behavior and ex- pression of the members of the group she is studying. Although it is not necessary to adopt such a practice, it is important to know what local norms and expectations for appearance are.

EXAMPLE 1.23

WHEN TO AVOID LOOKING LIKE A HIPPIE

LeCompte was assembling a team of interviewers for a study that explored why American Indian students in one high school had begun to experience significantly higher rates of failure in their classes than in previous years. The interviewers were recruited from among LeCompte's students, and the work required a stay of several days in the Navajo Nation. When she asked staff members at the Navajo school what specific advice she should give to the interviewers before they came, the high school librarian said, "I know that you all come from Boulder, Colorado, and that Boulder is the land of hippies. But Indian people down here don't like hippies. They are tired of all these blue-eyed blondes coming down in their cut-off jeans and Birkenstocks,[3] trying to live in teepees and acting like Indians when they don't know what they are doing. They are just trespassing. And they trash up sacred sites. So tell them: No long hair, no nose rings, and no Birkenstocks."

As important as adopting behavior that conforms to the standards of the host community can be, ethnographers also must be aware that trying to "act like Indians"—as in Example 1.23 above—can be as offensive as outright defiance of cultural norms.

THE IMPROPRIETY OF GOING NATIVE:
WHEN TO AVOID IMITATING RESEARCH PARTICIPANTS

A politically committed white female ethnographer was hired to coordinate an AIDS research project conducted among injection drug users in an urban area in the northeastern United States. Many of the staff members were African American or Latino. Anxious to learn more about the African American community, the coordinator began to spend long periods of time in households and community organizations and at public events in the black community, learning more and more about black culture. Soon, she began to use language and body movements that imitated those of her new friends and associates. At a staff meeting, the issue of cultural differences surfaced. Some black staff members strongly objected to what they perceived to be the coordinator's attempt to gain intimacy with black people by appropriating elements of a cultural experience that was not hers. The ethnographer explained that she was not aware that she had assumed these new behaviors and was only trying to show respect by learning more about black culture and communication styles. The team was able to resolve the conflict in an open discussion of the behaviors and what they meant to all members of the group.

➤•➤•➤

Culture, Class, and Education

Among the most important components of what ethnographers bring with them to the field are their patterns of behavior; beliefs about how the world does and should operate; preferences, skills, and ways of looking at the world that are shaped by our cultural heritage; social class; and educational levels. These aspects of identity profoundly affect presentation of self and, more importantly, expectations about how others should behave. Unfortunately, these components of identity often are those of which we are least aware; we take them for granted and believe them to have little effect on ourselves and others with whom we interact.

Class, in particular, is problematic. People from the middle and upper classes, who constitute many, if not most, of the people who direct research projects, have developed attitudes about work and responsibility, use of leisure time, and commitment to jobs that correspond to the kinds of middle- and upper-middle-class careers they pursue. They also have beliefs about standards of personal hygiene, punctuality, and appropriate dress that serve them well in their homes and on the job. In some cases, these attitudes derive from the relatively greater privilege that middle- and upper-class people enjoy in society. Such attitudes also are facilitated by the more stable, predictable, and hygienic conditions in which affluent people live. When researchers expect the people they study also to hold similar attitudes and beliefs, they may well be surprised, at best; at worst, they risk offending research participants by appearing to be elitist, snobbish, or simply ignorant of the realities of local living conditions.

EXAMPLE 1.25   ━●━●━

CLASS DIFFERENCES IN APPROACHES TO DENTAL CARE

Access to the lower-income community on the south side of Chicago where J. Schensul's educational intervention was located depended upon Schensul's relationship with the project's parent coordinator, an African American woman in her early forties from the community. Although generally positive, there were uneasy moments in their relationship, primarily because of class and educational differences between Schensul, a middle-class married professional with a PhD and older children, and the coordinator, a college-educated married woman with three children and a limited family income. These differences came into clear focus when the coordinator decided to have all her teeth pulled and replaced with dentures. Shocked, Schensul tried to convince her to repair—and save—her own teeth. The coordinator informed Schensul that dentures were a far preferable solution, not only because they were cheaper, but because they were permanent. The exchange made so vivid the differences in economic circumstances and perspective between Schensul and the coordinator that some time was required for the two team members to regain a comfortable level of communication.

━●━●━

CLASS AND ETHNIC DIFFERENCES IN WAYS TO RELAX

The director of an enrichment program for American Indian children often tried to have lunch with her Indian staff members so that they could, as the director said, "just be relaxed." She hoped that such events would build more closeness among the staff members. For the director, whose husband had a well-paying job and who came from an upper-class community in the eastern United States, a relaxing place was a restaurant with tables, cloth napkins, and waiters. For the Indian staff—most of whom were single parents struggling to meet expenses—such places were anything but relaxing. "Nice" restaurants were too expensive and reminded the Indian teachers of past patterns of discrimination that had precluded their even buying meals that they could carry out and eat at home. The Indian staff members also had short official lunch breaks; taking longer breaks to "relax" with the director meant falling behind in their daily duties. The director never understood why her staff members kept suggesting picnics in the park as an alternative, and neither the lunches nor the team building that the director wanted to organize ever occurred.

➤●➤●➤

Incidents such as these illustrate how people in the study community may prevent the ethnographer from accessing important information because they believe either that ethnographers will demonstrate too little sensitivity to the needs and lives of people in the community or that the conditions under which the information must be acquired violate standards for treatment to which they expect ethnographers to adhere.

COPING WITH ASSOCIATIONS IN THE FIELD: AFFILIATIONS, SPONSORSHIP, AND FRIENDS

Experienced ethnographers are aware that they are known by the company they keep. They know that they will bring personal and professional relationships into the field with them and acquire more of them once they have arrived; they also know that the existence of these relationships will affect how research participants intepret their behavior and motivations. They are aware that they will be affected by past history; in many cases, they will be expected to behave similarly to the previous researcher who visited the site, whether that researcher was viewed with favor or disfavor. We begin by discussing the impact of affiliations that researchers have before they enter the field.

The Impact of Institutional Affiliations and Sponsors

Initiation of any research project requires that ethnographers find people in the research site to grant them access and help them make initial contacts. We already have indicated that this necessary step in a research project can create problems for ethnographers, who cannot avoid being identified in some way with those who preceded them or who first introduce them to the community. However, the impact of these affiliations can, to some extent, be lessened. For example, ethnographers can organize their "presentation of self" (Goffman, 1959) so as to allay the fears that research participants have about what they might be like.

EXAMPLE 1.27

DRESSING TO CONTRADICT NEGATIVE STEREOTYPES

Medical anthropologist Stephen Schensul's first assignment from the medical school he represented was to build community placements for medical students by creating collaborative projects that linked the university medical school with agencies in the Hartford, Connecticut, area. Because the medical school had just moved from the city of Hartford to the suburbs, Hartford community residents felt betrayed, believing that its physicians and faculty had abandoned them. When Schensul first approached the heads of community agencies, they were reluctant to meet with him . . . until they saw his cowboy boots, blue jeans, and leather vest. Dubbing him the "cowboy anthropologist," they set aside their stereotypes of health center personnel and were able to establish more easily the collaborative research relationships that the community placements required.

Although Dr. Schensul was able to negate the community's negative stereotypes about his own institution, the negative impact of other kinds of affiliations and initial impressions are not so easily set aside, even when ethnographers spend extensive time in the community and make strenuous efforts to limit their effects.

━━•━•━━ **EXAMPLE 1.28**

WHEN THE WOUNDS OF HISTORY WILL NOT HEAL: WORKING WITH AN INTRACTABLE STEREOTYPE

LeCompte's work with a school district in "Pinnacle," an American Indian community, had been preceded by advice and counsel given by a parade of consultants and researchers. Each had charged substantial fees for their efforts, and few were described as very helpful by teachers and staff. By contrast, LeCompte received no fee or honorarium. The primary purpose of the grant she had written was to hire local people for several innovative programs designed to increase the number of Indians who were certified to teach in the local schools. The grant also provided scholarship money for several Indian teacher aides to complete their university training; it provided only travel and living expenses for LeCompte's monthly trips to the community. Notwithstanding the fact that LeCompte was not paid for her services, she still was viewed by many in the community as "one of those high-priced consultants" who came to the community "like used car salesmen. They all talk very loudly, don't tell us much that we could use, and then leave with their checks." This point of view, which had been established before she arrived in Pinnacle, colored the reception that LeCompte received and made some school staff unwilling to work with her.

Even before LeCompte arrived in Pinnacle, she was identified as a university-based researcher—like many of the previous consultants. Thus, she walked into a set of preconceptions about consultants that her predecessors had established. She also was identified as an educational reformer, because the first contact that many of the staff had with her was during the speech she was asked to give during beginning-of-the-year ceremonies. At the superintendent's request, she outlined in that talk a range of reform options in which the superintendent was interested. The speech made a number of teachers seriously uncomfortable because they had no desire to change how they taught. She also created some preconceptions during the talk by identifying herself with a particular set of school reforms. The latter identity could not be avoided; she was hired by the school district to help it implement those particular reforms. For some staff members, such an identity was a positive one; they had been very enthusiastic about the class that one of LeCompte's friends, an anthropologist familiar with the community, had taught in the district the year before. That class had been organized at the request of a group of the high school teachers to help them understand better the culture of the Indian students they taught. Unfortunately, LeCompte also earned some negative associations as a consequence of this class; her friend had hired LeCompte twice to come Pinnacle to help teach a unit on program evaluation. Those who resented LeCompte's presence interpreted both the speech and her evaluation workshop as indications that she might be called on to evaluate *them.*

━▪━▪━

All of these roles—consultant, educational reformer, evaluator—were real ones that LeCompte brought with her to the field. Even though she had been hired initially by the superintendent and then subsequently came to the district on funds she herself had procured for a program the superintendent wanted, her roles were confused by the way some district staff defined previous occupants of those roles—as shysters, con artists, or hired guns. Even people who did not hold these stereotypes tended to view her as a person whose ideas would increase the work overload that teachers already experienced. Differences between the roles as LeCompte defined them and the roles as they were defined by significant community members made it difficult for LeCompte to play other roles she found more desirable: collaborator, researcher, and colleague. Notwithstanding, ethnographers commonly balance—and carry out—all of these roles simultaneously, even though doing so is never easy and always fraught with tensions and ambivalence.

Personal Friendships in the Field

Ethnographers should be careful to delay establishing close relationships in the field or fully believing everything that initial informants tell them about the community. It is common for ethnographers to be befriended or "adopted" by atypical or eccentric individuals in the community who, lacking indigenous friends or support structures, seek legitimation or status in the company of the ethnographer. This can be a problem, because such people often are outcasts and certainly have idiosyncratic perspectives on the community. Furthermore, being known as a friend of such people may prevent developing contacts with other, more socially central, members of the community.

━•━•━　　　　　　　　**EXAMPLE 1.29**

THE DANGER OF BEING ASSOCIATED WITH MARGINAL GROUPS IN A COMMUNITY

An Anglo anthropologist in a large midwestern city joined a community research team whose mission was to establish relationships with a broad spectrum of community leaders and organizations. He was sought out by, and then befriended, two socially marginal left-wing community activists who were interested in building an interethnic political organization. The anthropologist became personally and politically involved with these two individuals, and his capacity to enter the Latino community with which the research team wished to work was, as a consequence, compromised to some degree. As a consequence, he was unable to fulfill his responsibilities as a member of the research team. In subsequent years, he still was perceived as associated with this small faction in the community even when he had moved on to other work.

━•━•━

Careful ethnographers take pains to befriend as many different kinds of people in the community as possible—thereby preserving the opportunity to create new contacts. They try to avoid creating enemies or being identified with specific factions.

EXAMPLE 1.30   ➤•➤•➤

AVOIDING NEGATIVE ROLES AND MAINTAINING OPEN COMMUNICATION

Niels Braroe, a Swedish anthropologist studying an Indian community in Canada, said,

> My wife and I [n]ever became identified as "Indian" (although I did become the adopted son of one couple and sibling to their children). Instead, since we could not be placed in any of the White roles familiar to Indians [and since we were not Indians, either], we were given a special place in the community. (Braroe, 1975, p. 22)

➤•➤•➤

Braroe's strategy permitted him to be situated as neither Indian nor white, but as sympathetic to the Indian point of view and uncritical of Indian behavior. He did not conform to beliefs among whites that Indians were dirty, lazy, and irresponsible. To be so positioned permitted Braroe to move to what is called the "back regions" (Goffman, 1959)—those behavior settings or parts of the social scene that normally would be inaccessible to outsiders. Such a location, although desirable, is sometimes impossible for the applied ethnographer to achieve because of affiliations and allegiances—real or imagined, as in the example of LeCompte's experience in Pinnacle—that the researcher brings to the field.

In the best cases, of course, the researcher's prior affiliations are viewed positively and serve to legitimate the presence of the ethnographer in the research site.

EXAMPLE 1.31

WHEN INFORMANTS THINK RESEARCHERS' PRIOR AFFILIATIONS ARE BENEFICIAL

When LeCompte presented her proposal for a collaborative evaluation of the Arts Enrichment Program to Edgecliff Middle School's faculty and staff, she met with unexpected enthusiasm from the principal of the school. "We are the only enrichment program in the district that will have its own researcher," he said. "We really are lucky to have Dr. LeCompte work with us, because she's a link to the university and its resources." Within several weeks, the principal and his assistant had found several ways to assist with LeCompte's data collection. In return, he solicited LeCompte's advice in locating consultants, securing financial support from foundations for the Arts Enrichment and other programs, and gaining access to the university's art gallery for student field trips.

FORMAL AND SEMIFORMAL RESPONSIBILITIES: INSTITUTIONAL REVIEW BOARDS, CONTRACTS, AND GOOD MANNERS

Up to now, we have been talking about the personal characteristics and more or less informal affiliations of researchers, how these affect the way ethnographers present themselves to others, and how they are presented and represented by others in their research sites. Equally important are formal and semiformal responsibilities inherent in much ethnographic research.

Formal Responsibilities

Formal responsibilities and obligations are those that dictate what kind of data will be collected, how and where data will be stored, how the people who are targets of research are to be treated from an ethical standpoint, and how they will be protected from undue risks or breaches of privacy stemming from their participation in the study. They also dictate how much time the researcher has to complete the task, how and for what purposes funds will be disbursed and to whom, and when results will be disseminated. Often, formal responsibilities include the specific ways in which research results will be presented to various audiences, including requirements that the researcher provide ongoing feedback to research participants or partners while the study is in progress. These responsibilities most frequently are the product of negotiation between agencies and the researcher(s); researchers are brought into a setting as resources who can help foundations, institutions, agencies, or individuals design the most appropriate, effective, and efficient way to answer research questions and solve problems. In the research design part of Book 1, we spelled out a variety of ways in which researchers design investigations. These designs, in effect, are the blueprints for contractual relationships and responsibilities. Because researchers usually constrain their designs within very broad guidelines, they actually have a good deal of voice in defining the responsibilities that they will be called upon to carry out. Notwithstanding, once they *are* spelled out and the contracts are signed, the responsibilities are binding.

Cross Reference: See Book 1, Chapter 4, on research design

Formal responsibilities and obligations also exist in the rules imposed on researchers by governments and the codes of ethics that govern the appropriate behavior of researchers vis-à-vis other human beings with whom they work and interact in research settings. Other formal responsibilities are contractual or ethical ones embedded in the tasks researchers have been hired or asked to do; these can be written into contracts, depending upon specific agreements.

Constraints on or responsibilities for researcher behavior imposed by the political culture or governmental edicts at the research site often are taken for granted when researchers do their work within their own country. Most researchers in the United States, for example, are aware of guidelines for the ethical treatment of human participants in research studies to which all investigators are held responsible. However, researchers may be unaware of quite real guidelines that they follow scrupulously because such guidelines constitute the givens of ordinary good practice within their own society; for the most part, such givens may not be appreciated, but they are at least understood. They include such things as not lying to, or stealing from, research participants; not falsifying data to make them conform to the researcher's own expectations or theories; and being sure to have plans for disseminating data. University researchers, for example, generally include dissemination plans, if only because publication or presentation of research results is required for career advancement. Similarly, medical researchers do not use contaminated materials, not only because they might contaminate research results, but because they might be harmful to participants.

Lack of knowledge or awareness of governmental constraints can create significant problems for researchers, whether or not they work outside their own country. Researchers may, for example, be unaware of the guidelines for treatment of certain types of human subjects. The U.S. Office for Protection from Research Risks (OPRR) requires that special protections be established for interviewing prisoners and other people in custodial institutions, including anyone under the jurisdiction of the justice system. This can include people who are on judicial probation or parole, or those engaged in punitive alternatives to incarceration. Without reading the guidelines, researchers might fail to put into place those special protections, thereby unwittingly exposing people in custody to unwarranted risk.

More problematic are those cases where researchers deliberately circumvent or violate explicit or implicit government rules about what they may or may not study and what information they may disseminate. A notorious case was the doctoral dissertation research of Steven Mosher, a graduate student from Stanford University.

EXAMPLE 1.32   ➤•➤•➤

DELIBERATE VIOLATION OF FORMAL RULES REGARDING RESEARCH CONDUCT

Mosher proposed to study methods of birth control and contraception in the People's Republic of China during the late 1960s. Both Stanford University's Department of Anthropology and the government of China agreed to his project, but the Chinese government stipulated that he was not to talk about, collect data on, or explore the use of birth control techniques to select the sex of children. Most especially, Mosher was not to investigate possible instances of female infanticide. Mosher was, however, approached by American groups that were strongly opposed to the practice of abortion and encouraged by them to expose what they believed to be the widespread occurrence of female infanticide in China. Mosher agreed and carried out these investigations in violation of his agreements with Stanford and the Chinese government. Although a commercial press eventually published his findings, Stanford University refused to approve his dissertation research, and he did not receive his PhD.

➤•➤•➤

Institutional Review Boards or Committees Governing the Treatment of Human Research Subjects

Key point   *In many countries, the rules and regulations for conduct of research are not codified. This means that researchers must be particularly careful to engage in preliminary planning and fieldwork to find out what obstacles they might encounter before they embark on a project.* However, in the United States, the Code of Federal Regulations (CFR), which codifies all administrative regulations promulgated by agencies of the federal government, spells out in detail the requirements that the Department of Health and Human Services has established for the treatment of human research subjects. These guidelines, which must be applied to research conducted by researchers from American institutions—regardless of whether the work is done within or outside of the country—generally fall into five areas:

- Protection of human subjects of research against undue and unnecessary risks from participation in research
- Assurance that everyone participating as a subject in research has consented to participation and understands what the researcher plans to do with them and with the research data
- Assurance that the privacy of the research subject will be protected
- A guarantee that participants in research know who is doing the research and how to contact the researchers if they have questions or problems with their participation in the study
- Guarantees that special care be taken when research is carried out on or among **vulnerable populations**

Definition:
A vulnerable population consists of people who cannot consent freely to participation in a research project because they would incur unnecessary risks, experience possible coercion, or be unable to understand the risks or procedures involved

The Code of Federal Regulations has mandated these assurances for a number of reasons. *First, the United States government has taken responsibility for enforcing rules about informed consent to make sure that human beings do not become participants in research projects unwillingly or without their knowledge. Second, people must be informed about and fully understand what the research entails before consent can be considered legitimate.* People who cannot understand the research procedures cannot be well enough informed to legitimately give consent for participation. Furthermore, research always involves certain risks and benefits; some projects may be riskier than others. *Participation in research projects involves greater risk for certain types of people than it does for others.* To protect the latter, the CFR has defined categories of vulnerable populations for whom special consideration must be given.

Key point

Key point

*Types of Vulnerable Populations Defined
by the Code of Federal Regulations*

- Mentally handicapped people
- Children under the age of 18
- Incarcerated or institutionalized people
- People who are illiterate or who do not speak the dominant language of the culture or the language of the researcher
- People whose participation in a research project would expose their own illegal status or activities and thereby cause them to risk arrest and imprisonment
- People who are ill or physically handicapped, and women who are pregnant
  — If the research has to do with their physical condition
  — If the potential participants feel pressure to participate in the research in order to receive or continue with treatment that they need or want and cannot otherwise obtain

Research that involves vulnerable populations invites special scrutiny and calls for special responsibilities on the part of the researcher, as does research that could pose physical, emotional, social, or financial risk to participants; involves statuses or behavior considered dangerous to others; or concerns behavior that is stigmatized or illegal in the society where the study is located. Examples of research that could be risky or dangerous to participants include studies that investigate the following:

- The behavior of people who use drugs in a society that designates those drugs to be illegal
- Immigrant teenaged dropouts, some of whose parents might be illegal residents subject to deportation
- Doctor/client interactions in an abortion clinic, where clients might feel as though failure to participate in the research project could jeopardize their ability to obtain an abortion

Sometimes, even procedures used to select research participants can be viewed as risky or coercive if they are carried out by people who are in a superior relationship to the potential participants. For example, juveniles charged with criminal behavior might feel that they would encounter reprisals if they refused to participate in a research study when asked to do so by a social worker, probation officer, or other employee of the juvenile justice system that supervised their punishment. Students whose teacher was trying to evaluate the effectiveness of an innovation also might feel coerced to participate in a study on the grounds that refusal to participate could affect their grades.

Even the general requirement that researchers obtain signed consent forms from all participants in a research study can, in fact, endanger people engaged in illegal or tabooed activities if the only way that such people could be identified were through the seizure of the researcher's consent forms.

The CFR originally required that every institution carrying out research with human subjects establish an institutional review board that, in turn, was required to approve all research done by researchers receiving federal funds to carry out their research. The IRB was charged with guaranteeing that researchers adhere to the CFR's requirements. In practice, most IRBs review all research projects whether or not they receive federal funds, because most institutions housing researchers do, in fact, receive some kind of federal subsidy or grant. The work of any researcher working in or with such a federally subsidized institution falls under the jurisdiction of that institution's IRB.

Institutional review boards are routinely established by universities, research institutions, and medical facilities; often foundations, funding agencies, human service agencies, and school districts establish them as well. IRBs are required to establish and make public their own procedures for approving research studies. Obtaining approval usually involves submitting a written proposal to the IRB, which will then review and approve or disapprove the study. Normally, research cannot begin until approval is obtained.

IRBs establish a whole set of responsibilities for researchers. IRBs are concerned that people who agree to participate in research should not be subject to harm unless the harm is justified by the value of the research and unless participants fully understand what they are agreeing to do. Unlike medical researchers, ethnographers do not often engage in research that is potentially dangerous to the physical health of research participants. *However, ethnographies often receive particularly stringent scrutiny by IRBs because anonymity of participants in ethnographic research is particularly difficult to maintain.* IRB scrutiny is justified on the basis of the potential harm that might be done to research participants if their confidentiality, anonymity, or privacy were breached. Relationships between people in the research site and the researcher are close and frequent, and participants are, as a consequence, known well by the researcher. In addition, the social dynamics that form a good part of many ethnographic descriptions include descriptions of particular individuals whose identity is difficult to disguise completely. Particular unique individuals, events, communities, or institutions sometimes cannot be described at all without providing some markers that would clearly disclose who or what was under investigation. Furthermore, even if ethnographers do use pseudonyms and disguise their informants' identities in other ways, researchers can be forced by law to disclose who their research subjects are if those individuals are suspected of, or known to have been, engaging in illegal activities unless they receive special governmental protection for the study and its participants. This protection is called a certificate of confidentiality; we discuss it later. The ethnographer's task, then, is particularly difficult. What do ethnographers do to obtain IRB approval?

 Key point

Gaining IRB Approval for Research

Most IRBs are not very concerned with the theoretical or conceptual framework of the research, or even if anyone else has done similar studies—unless the fact that other people have used the same procedures without harming subjects forms the researcher's justification for a particular approach. *IRBs principally want to know how researchers* **Key point** *selected their participants, what they plan to do to them, how they plan to protect participants' privacy, and how informed consent is to be obtained.* As a result, the proposals that researchers submit for approval to IRBs generally do not have to be as lengthy as those provided for other kinds of agencies, but they must spell out in detail at least the following:

> ### Components of an Application for IRB Approval
>
> - A description of what the researcher plans to do with the research participants. For example, the researcher might say that he or she planned to observe children in classrooms and on the playgrounds, audiotape interviews with them, collect the results of their standardized tests, and ask them to role-play an imaginary interaction with their teacher that the researcher would videotape.
>
> - A description of the data collection methods to be used, including lists of questions or topics to be asked about in interviews and copies of questionnaires, tests, or other instruments that are to be used.
>
> - Copies of letters to be sent to research participants, explaining the research study and asking for the consent of individuals whom the researcher wanted to study. Normally, these letters must be signed to indicate consent, although under certain circumstances, consent can be given by legal guardians, and in very special circumstances, written consent can be waived, especially if the letter of consent serves as the only way to identify participants in sensitive or illegal activities.

- Copies of letters from institutions, schools, hospitals, clinics, youth centers, or any other organization where potential subjects are to be located, indicating that the organization supports the researcher's project and agrees to provide access to the site and the target population.
- Information about the qualifications of the researchers, as well as how to contact them by telephone, mail, fax, e-mail, or other means.
- A description of the ways in which the researcher plans to protect the identity or privacy of the people who participate in the study, and what will be done with the data when the study is complete.
- A description of the risks and benefits that participation in the project would bring to the research subjects.
- A description of how the researcher plans to help the participants ameliorate any adverse effects of participating in the project, if risks are present.

Researchers are required to provide all of the above-listed information to potential research participants in abbreviated form and in language that is understandable to the participants. Usually, this is done in the form of letters read by or read to participants that explain the research and ask them to consent to participation in the research. These letters, referred to as **consent forms**, must make very clear to the research participants what they will be expected to do and how their identity will be kept confidential or protected. At the end of this chapter, we provide some examples of informed consent letters and the kinds of guidelines that IRBs provide to researchers.

 Definition: Consent forms are letters of agreement to participate in a study that inform participants of what will happen to them, risks and benefits, and whom to contact for questions

There are some exceptions to the rules about protecting identity. It is not necessary for researchers to disguise the identity of specific public figures, particularly elected officials, who, it is presumed, have waived the right to anonymity at least with respect to their public actions. In cases where a written consent form would be the only way that the research participant's identity would be known, and the knowledge of that identity might prove risky to the participant, researchers can ask for a waiver to the customary written consent. In certain limited instances involving research that might disclose illegal activity by research participants, ethnographers can obtain a Writ of Protection or a Certificate of Confidentiality from the U.S. government. Such a Writ or Certificate assures both the researcher and the research subject that the information gathered by the researcher is privileged; that is, the government—including agencies such as the police—agrees that it will not subpoena or seize the researcher's data in order to find out the identity of the researcher's subjects. The Certificate of Confidentiality is obtained by preparing for submission to the Federal Office for Protection from Research Risks (OPRR) a package of information in accordance with their guidelines, including description of the target population; sample size and sampling procedures; required statements of assurance from the researcher's home institution that it reviews research in accordance with U.S. government regulations; copies of approved consent forms; and the statement of acceptance of the plan for protection of human subjects approved by the IRB of the researcher's home institution, the grantee organization (if any), and its grant review committee.

An exception to these stringent requirements involves research that uses data collected in such a way that no individuals can be identified—such as anonymous, mailed surveys. Examples can include sensitive data if they cannot be linked to specific people. Examples might include data about the prevalence of HIV/AIDS obtained from blood samples taken from newborn babies, if the only data associated with the samples were gender and race of the baby and the location of hospitals where the samples were collected.

A further exception to the requirement to obtain IRB approval involves certain kinds of institutional research.

Such research is done by researchers hired or employed by an agency to study its own programs, employees, or clients. Under these conditions, employees can be required to participate, but the clients should be asked by researchers for permission to use data from their particular cases—if it would permit them to be identified individually—and they also should be given the opportunity not to participate if they so choose. Of course, research using publicly available archives and documents generally requires no IRB approval at all.

Cross Reference: See Book 2, Chapter 9, for more information on archival and secondary data

The Power of IRBs

Institutional review boards are responsible not only for reviewing and approving new projects, but also for conducting annual reviews of ongoing projects. Annual reviews require researchers to report:

- Whether the research procedures have changed
- Whether the research has had any adverse effects on participants
- How the adverse effects—if any—have been treated, and what researchers have done to ensure that such effects do not occur again
- What results, if any, have been obtained.

Key point Such reports normally are brief but important. *IRBs have the power to require changes in research projects to make them less risky for subjects, to disapprove new projects, to stop ongoing projects, or to prevent researchers from publishing or using data from completed projects if researchers do not obtain appropriate approvals and conform to the general guidelines concerning ethical treatment of research participants and the specific terms of their own approval agreement negotiated with the IRB.* IRBs also are authorized to approve or disapprove research taking place outside the United States if the researchers are U.S. citizens or legal residents, or if they

are working with or under the auspices of institutions lo-
cated in the United States. Thus, *even non-U.S. citizens doing*   **Key point**
research in their own countries must conform to IRB guide-
lines if the institution sponsoring the research or housing the
researcher is located in the United States.

Contracts With Funding Agencies

Funding agencies and researchers initiate mutual responsibilities when researchers respond to requests for proposals that funding agencies develop to provide the framework for investigations they want researchers to carry out.
The **requests for proposals** (RFPs) spell out the specific   **Definition:**
areas to which the research should be addressed or pro-   A request for
grams that should be studied, the time period for which   proposal (RFP) is
the announcement
funding will be provided, the categories of individuals or   funding agencies
groups eligible to compete or apply for funds, and how   produce outlining
much money will be available for specific projects. They   guidelines for
may specify the research design—for example, ethnogra-   research they wish
to have investigators
phy, surveys, or studies that, because program impact is   carry out
desired, require experimental designs—target populations
or specific sites to be investigated, partnership organizations that must be included as participants, qualifications
of the researcher(s), plans for dissemination of results, and
a variety of other stipulations. They can call for cooperative
agreements with specific organizations or groups.

Proposals that respond to RFPs include detailed information as to how the researcher plans to conform to these
stipulations. The proposals, if accepted, constitute a kind of
contract between researcher and funding agencies that de-
lineates quite a few of the responsibilities that the researcher
must carry out in the course of the study. The time lines and
data-planning matrices found in Book 1, Chapter 6, are
examples of how a researcher responded systematically to
one set of RFP requirements.

Contracts With Governmental
and Nongovernmental Agencies

Contracts with governmental or nongovernmental agencies or nonprofit organizations is much like contracts with a funding source, although they probably will not be as detailed. All such contracts establish a range of responsibilities for researchers. Normally, these contracts spell out the topics or questions that the researcher is to investigate, how much time is available for the research, and the resources to be allocated to the study. Often, the contract specifies where and with whom the researcher will be expected to work and how and to whom the research results will be disseminated. They also can clarify what researchers can and cannot do.

The Researcher's
Informal Responsibilities

Informal responsibilities are embedded in norms governing how people are supposed to act within the particular web of social affiliations and interaction at the sites and among the research partnerships where the research is located. We discuss these as they apply to individual researchers in this chapter. How they affect research teams and partnerships is addressed more fully in Chapter 2.

Most informal responsibilities are unlikely to be codified or written down. However, they are deeply embedded in rules, expectations, and obligations governing the culture, setting, or context of the investigation. Such responsibilities often can be subsumed under the heading of "good manners" or proper etiquette; more formally, they constitute the web of politeness, sensitivity, and proper demeanor that maintain good interpersonal relationships in any social setting. In the research context, they consist of the following:

- Representing appropriately the organization that has hired the researchers, so as to ensure the continuing good reputation of the organization (as well as other researchers) in that particular setting
- Respecting the values and norms of the country or community in which the research site is located, even if the researcher does not agree with them
- Showing respect for other researchers, even if their methods or approaches differ from the researcher's own
- Learning how to be polite in the culture of the research site
- Practicing reciprocity and sharing ideas, resources, and responsibilities
- Helping out in small ways with activities in the community or participant organization on a daily basis

Implicit in these rules of "manners" are other rules that more closely resemble ethical imperatives vis-à-vis research participants and staff members in partnership organizations. These include the following:

- Not sharing or disclosing information that could adversely affect the lives of others
- Being aware that researchers may not be able to distinguish information that could be harmful from that which is not
- Keeping in mind the right of participants in the research site to review beforehand what will be said in reports, whether oral or written
- Involving people from the research site in interpretation and analysis of data so that their voices are heard
- Publishing reports in the country or community in which the research project is located
- Contributing income or comparable resources where large class or wealth discrepancies exist between researchers and community participants

Most of these informal expectations are spelled out in the codes of ethics supported by each social science discipline's professional organization.

THE ROLE OF REFLECTION IN ETHNOGRAPHIC RESEARCH

 Definition: Disciplined subjectivity is the practice of rigorous self-reflection about one's own impact on the field, as well as how one's preferences, prejudices, biases, hopes, and concerns affect the course and outcomes of research

One of the most important roles that the ethnographer plays, both in the field and outside of it, is what one could call "self-interrogator," or someone who constantly holds his or her own opinions, conclusions, and beliefs about what has happened in the field site up for inspection to ensure that they are valid. Doing so requires what theorists call **"disciplined subjectivity"** (Erickson, 1985/1986), or the practice of rigorous self-reflection about one's own preferences, prejudices, hopes, and concerns; it serves as a necessary practice for all careful ethnographers, as well as a check on misinterpretations. We encourage this kind of systematic self-reflection before, during, and after the field experience.

Before entering the field, ethnographers should establish the practice of learning as much as possible about the field setting. Through this process, they are able to identify cultural practices and values that could be discomforting to them or that might challenge their values and ways of viewing the world. They should also identify biases, prejudices, and patterns of thought that, although they are taken for granted, actually constitute culturally specific ways of viewing the world and the beliefs and behaviors of others that could jeopardize their ability to see clearly in the field. Self-reflection also can help ethnographers identify their commitments to specific research topics and outcomes, as well as the potential that such behaviors might have for biasing or negatively influencing research results. For example, researchers can ask themselves what is most important to them about their research, what they hope (rather than hypothesize) to find, and what they believe is wrong about the setting or the behavior of the people in it. From these questions, they can begin to identify personal viewpoints that might keep them from obtaining a well-rounded set of data for analysis and to ask questions that can counter these prejudices and expand their database.

Once in the field, ethnographers should continue to engage in a scrupulous review of all of their personal characteristics and foibles, seen in the light of real acquaintance with people in the field, to enumerate how these might affect their interactions with research participants. This can include the use of a variety of strategies to help ethnographers maintain the practice of disciplined subjectivity throughout their study.

Strategies for Practicing Disciplined Subjectivity

- Create a checklist of all of one's prior hunches and theoretical biases and examining them regularly to see if they are leading the data collection and analysis in ways not warranted by what actually occurs in the field
- Maintain personal logs and observations
- Keep diaries and journals
- Write letters "home" that may or may not actually be sent, but that, because they are written ostensibly for an outside reader, can summarize the field experience from a personal point of view
- Create reflexive accounts—accounts of the fieldworker's thoughts and reactions that parallel the descriptions of what he or she has observed in the field. Reflexive accounts are written from an affective, or subjective and emotional, perspective rather than from one that simply seeks to record what happens
- Review one's own theoretical underpinnings as well as one's personal preferences. These can be conceptualized as "hot" and "cold" spots (Peshkin 1988), or those aspects of fieldwork toward which one is drawn and therefore spends more time exploring (the hot spots) and those that one tends to dislike or feel uncomfortable with and therefore spends less time exploring (the cold spots)
- Monitor the small disjunctures in behavior or communication between researcher and participants that signify the researcher has violated cultural norms in the field site

■ Solicit the help of mentors or other professionals who are not connected to the research project to read review data; examine analysis strategies and interpretations; and provide feedback on areas that might need more attention, those that are overemphasized to the exclusion of other important topics, and conclusions that the researcher has missed, inflated, or arrived at prematurely

■ Create a formal review panel, funded by the project budget, to act as outside consultants whose tasks are similar to those of volunteer mentors and colleagues described above

■ Solicit the help of key informants in the field to review data, data collection strategies, analysis procedures, and intepretations to identify similar omissions and commissions not intended by the researcher or deleterious to an authentic portrayal of the cultural scene under study.

EXAMPLE 1.33   ➤•➤•➤

DISCOVERING A COLD SPOT

LeCompte found the Director of Special Programs in one district where she was a consultant to be very difficult to work with. Many of the tasks needed for the implementation of the programs that LeCompte was to set up required the cooperation of the director. However, although the director always was affable and seemed amenable to their joint project, her staff never seemed to accomplish the tasks that the director and LeCompte agreed to share among their respective teams. The director's passive resistance to the innovative projects that LeCompte was initiating was described by one of LeCompte's research team members as "trying to batter down a wall of feathers"; arrangements that were set up fell through, materials that were to be ordered never came, and rooms that were to be available were already booked when the research team arrived. Although LeCompte was exhorted by the superintendent just to keep working with the director, she began to avoid the informal meetings and conversations with the director that she held regularly with all of the other staff members in the district. It seemed too uncomfortable to continue trying to collaborate when all she could think of were the many times that cooperation had failed.

➤•➤•➤

Once the researcher has left the field, it is especially important to implement strategies that will provide a counterpoint or check on the researcher's own theoretical or conceptual leanings. Some of the same strategies used in the field can be put to good use during the data analysis and interpretation phases of the study. These include soliciting feedback on preliminary conclusions and interpretations from key informants and knowledgeable outsiders, including one's mentors and other professionals in the field. However the reflection process is initiated, its systematic use ensures not only that the final reports will be authentic representations of the cultural scene that the study was intended to portray, but also that the entire study will have the sheen of rigorous implementation. In the final book in this series, several noted ethnographers describe how such studies can be used in planning, implementing, and evaluating culturally appropriate and innovative programs, and also in using ethnographic research to influence public policy.

Cross Reference:
See Book 1 for a discussion of ways ethnographers can say goodbye to people in their research sites

Cross Reference:
See Book 5 for a discussion of ways in which researchers control for their own biases when interpreting data

NOTES

1. The term "embedded contexts" is taken from Cole and Griffin (1992); we have adapted their scheme for more general use.
2. The writer is, in fact, from Sweden.
3. Birkenstocks are a kind of sandal made in Germany and popular among young people in the United States. In the 1970s, Birkenstocks were a symbol of countercultural, or hippie, lifestyles.

REFERENCES

Bernard, H. R. (1995). *Research methods in anthropology: Qualitative and quantitative approaches* (2nd ed.). Walnut Creek, CA: AltaMira.

Bolton, R. (1995). Tricks, friends and lovers: Erotic encounters in the field. In D. Kulick & M. Willson (Eds.), *Taboo, sex identity and erotic subjectivity in anthropological fieldwork*. London: Routledge.

Braroe, N. L. (1975). *Indian and white: Self-image and interaction in a Canadian Plains community*. Stanford, CA: Stanford University Press.

Burnett, J. H. (1974). On the analog between culture acquisition and ethnographic method. *Anthropology and Education Quarterly, 5*(1), 25-29.

Cole, M., & Griffen, P. (Eds.). *Contextual factors in education: Improving science and mathematics education for minorities and women.* Madison, WI: Wisconsin Center for Educational Research.

Deyhle, D. M. (1986). Break dancing and breaking out: Anglos, Utes, and Navajos in a border reservation school. *Anthropology and Education Quarterly, 17,* 111-127.

Erickson, F. (1985/1986). Qualitative methods in research on teaching. In M. C. Wittrock (Ed.), *The handbook of research in teaching* (3rd ed., pp. 119-161). New York: Macmillan.

Goffman, E. (1959). *The presentation of self in everyday life.* Garden City, NY: Doubleday.

Goffman, E. (1961). *Asylums: Essays on the social situation of mental patients and other inmates.* Garden City, NY: Doubleday-Anchor.

Hartsock, N. C. M. (1983). The feminist standpoint: Developing the ground for a specifically feminist historical materialism. In S. Harding & M. Hintikka (Eds.), *Discovering reality: Feminist perspectives on epistemology, metaphysics, methodology and philosophy of science.* Boston: Reidel.

Heath, S. B. (1996, September 30). *Postmodern narrative and its consequences in knowledge transition.* Lecture 1, School of Education, University of Colorado.

Humphries, L. (1970a). *Tea room trade.* Chicago: Aldine.

Humphries, L. (1970b, January). Tea room trade: Impersonal sex in public places. *Transaction,* pp. 10-26.

Lather, P. (1986). Research as praxis. *Harvard Educational Review, 56,* 257-277.

LeCompte, M. D., & Preissle, J., with Tesch, R. (1993). *Ethnography and qualitative design in educational research* (2nd ed.). San Diego, CA: Academic Press.

Mead, M. (1928). *Coming of age in Samoa: A psychological study of primitive youth for Western civilization.* New York: Morrow.

Metz, M. H. (1978). *Classrooms and corridors: The crisis of authority in desegregated secondary schools.* Berkeley: University of California Press.

Pelto, P. J., & Pelto, G. H. (1978). *Anthropological research: The structure of inquiry* (2nd ed.). Cambridge, UK: Cambridge University Press.

Peshkin, A. (1988, October). Discovering subjectivities: One's own. *Educational Researcher,* pp. 17-21.

Powdermaker, H. (1966). *Stranger and friend: The way of an anthropologist.* New York: Norton.

Roman, L. G. (1988). Intimacy, labor and class: Ideologies of feminine sexuality in the Punk slam dance. In L. G. Roman & L. Christian-Smith (Eds.), *Becoming feminine: The politics of popular culture* (pp. 148-170). London: Falmer.

Roman, L. G. (1992). The political significance of other ways of narrating ethnography: A feminist materialist approach. In M. D. LeCompte, W. L. Millroy, & J. Preissle (Eds.), *The handbook of qualitative research in education* (pp. 555-594). San Diego, CA: Academic Press.

Roman, L. G. (1993). Double exposure: The politics of feminist materialist ethnography. *Educational Theory, 43,* 278-309.

Schensul, S., & Schensul, J. (1978). Advocacy and applied anthropology. In G. Weber & G. McCall (Eds.), *Social scientists as advocates: Views from the applied disciplines.* Beverly Hills, CA: Sage.

Silva, K. T., Schensul, S., Schensul, J., de Silva, A., Nastasi, B. K., Sivayo-ganathan, C., Lewis, J., Wedisinghe, P., Ratnayake, P., Eisenberg, M., & Aponso, H. (1997). *Youth and sexual risk in Sri Lanka.* Phase II Report Series, International Center for Research on Women, Washington, DC.

Spradley, J. P. (1979). *The ethnographic interview.* New York: Holt, Rinehart & Winston.

Wax, R. (1971). *Doing fieldwork: Warnings and advice.* Chicago: University of Chicago Press.

Weller, S. C., & Romney, A. K. (1988). *Systematic data collection.* Newbury Park, CA: Sage.

Werner, O., & Schoepfle, G. M. (1987a). *Systematic fieldwork* (Vol. 1). Newbury Park, CA: Sage.

Werner, O., & Schoepfle, G. M. (1987b). *Systematic fieldwork* (Vol. 2). Newbury Park, CA: Sage.

APPENDIX A

Parental Consent Form for
Students in the Arts Focus Program

A letter of this nature is required whenever a minor child or someone for whom a guardian has been appointed is to be a participant in a research study. The letters explain in detail the purpose of the study, the data to be collected, what will happen to the child if he or she participates in the study, how confidentiality will be protected, and the risks and benefits of participation. The letter also gives the names of researchers and their sponsors and ways to contact them if participants have questions or concerns.

Informed Consent Form for:

"Imagining the Future, Creating the Present: The Impact of Arts Education on Achievement and Identity in Arts Focus" (for the parents of Arts Focus students)

We are inviting your child to participate in the study that we have been conducting of the Arts Focus Program. We are Margaret (Marki) LeCompte, a faculty member at the University of Colorado, School of Education, and Debra Holloway, a doctoral student in the School of Education. Our school address is the University of Colorado, School of Education, Campus Box 249, Boulder, CO 80309-0249. If you would like to reach either Marki or Debra to talk about this project, feel free to call us. You can reach Marki at (303) 492-7951.

For the past two years, we have conducted an evaluation of the Arts Focus Program for Base Line Middle School. We have felt that it is important to include the experiences of the Arts Focus students in this evaluation of the program. We have been interested in how the program affects students and how it may change the role relationships and the patterns of learning in Arts Focus classes. We also are interested in how such changes affect student achievement, how children feel about school, and what they want to be when they grow up. This year, we want to continue studying the program and its impact on students through observation and interviews.

We would like to observe your child during his or her Arts Focus classes and on fieldtrips. During these observations, we will be taking notes on the interaction patterns among students and teachers as well as their activities in the classroom and the community.

We also would like to talk to your child(ren) about his or her experiences in the Arts Focus Program and audiotape the interview. The interview should take approximately 45 minutes to an hour, depending on how much your child has to say. We will be happy to meet with your child(ren) when and wherever is convenient for you. We will be tape-recording our conversations with students to ensure that we remember exactly what was said, but we will assign codes to each tape and its transcript and will delete any references to individual students' names. Once we have completed the project, we will erase the audiotapes. All data will be kept in locked cabinets at the home of Marki LeCompte, Project Director, and Debra Holloway, Research Assistant.

In order to study the long-term effects of the program, we have started building a database on Arts Focus students' achievement and would like to include your child(ren)'s standardized test scores and semester grades in it. We also would like to include information on student growth from portfolios and journals. We can assess student growth only by comparing the grades and scores of students over time. For this reason, we are asking for permission to enter your child(ren)'s yearly achievement data into our confidential database, including last year's information. To ensure confidentiality, Mike Morris, the Principal at Base Line, will assign a code number to your child's academic record. Data from these coded records will be entered into our database and followed while your child is at Base Line to assess whether involvement in Arts Focus affects academic achievement. Mr. Morris will keep the master list of codes and student names in his office at all times; no data that could identify a specific child's achievement will ever leave the school building.

We do not believe that there are any risks associated with participation in this project. The Arts Focus Program and Base Line Middle School will, however, benefit from evaluation and feedback that will help improve the program. Your child(ren) may gain insight into why he or she has experienced successes and/or frustrations in the program. He or she may enjoy contributing to the improvement of the program based on the evaluation.

We also have enclosed a survey for Arts Focus parents. We want to know how you feel about the program, what your interests and background in the arts might be, and what successes and problems have occurred in the program this year. You are not asked to include your name on the survey. Please return it along with the consent and assent forms in the envelope provided.

If you and your child(ren) decide to participate in this project, please understand that your participation is voluntary and that both you and s/he have the right to withdraw your consent or to discontinue participation at any time. Both you and s/he has the right to refuse to answer any question(s) for any reason. Also, your and your child(ren)'s individual privacy will be maintained in all published and written material resulting from this study. We will use pseudonyms to disguise the identity of all participants.

If you have any questions regarding your child(ren)'s rights as a participant, any concerns regarding this project, or any dissatisfaction with any part of this study, you may report them to us or—confidentially, if you wish—to the Executive Secretary, Human Research Committee, Graduate School, Campus Box 26, Regent 309, University of Colorado, Boulder, CO 80309-0026, or you may call (303) 492-7401 and speak directly to the Executive Secretary. Copies of the University of Colorado Assurance of Compliance to the federal government regarding human subjects research are available upon request from the Graduate School address listed below.

Please sign both of these consent forms. One is for you, and the other (next page) is for our records. Please sign the next page and enclose it along with your child(ren)'s assent form in the self-addressed stamped envelope provided.

Thank you.

I understand the above information and voluntarily consent to let my child(ren) participate in the study titled "Imagining the Future, Creating the Present: The Impact of Arts Education on Achievement and Identity in Arts Focus."

Signature of Parent _____ *Date* _____

Please print your child(ren)'s full name(s)

_____

Please circle child(ren)'s grade(s):   6th   7th   8th

Please circle child(ren)'s Arts Focus area(s):   Visual   Theatre/Dance   Instrumental Music

APPENDIX B

Assent Form for Arts Focus Students (aged 10-15)

A letter of assent is also required for minor children and people who are under guardianship if they are deemed capable of understanding the procedures of the research and the purposes of the study. Generally, normal children can give assent after the age of 5 or 6; the letters, however, must be written carefully so that their language is understandable to the child. A researcher cannot use as a participant any child for whom he or she does not have both the parents' and the child's consent.

Assent Form for:

"Imagining the Future, Creating the Present: The Impact of Arts Education on Achievement and Identity in Arts Focus" (for students involved in the Arts Focus Program)

We want to invite you to help us in our study of the Arts Focus Program. We are Marki LeCompte, a faculty member at the University of Colorado, and Debra Holloway, a student at the University of Colorado, and this will be our third year of studying the impact on of the program on students. If you ever want to talk to either of us about this project, you may contact us at the University of Colorado, School of Education, Campus Box 249, Boulder, CO 80309-0249, or call Marki at (303) 492-7951.

For the past two years, we evaluated the Arts Focus program for Base Line Middle School. We believe it is important to include your experiences as an Arts Focus student in our studies. This year, we want to continue studying the program and its influence on you. We are interested in what you are learning in the Arts Focus Program and how the Arts Focus Program influences you personally and academically.

We may observe you during your Arts Focus classes and on field trips. During these occasions, we will take notes on the ways students and teachers talk to each other and on their activities. We also would like to include your standardized test scores, semester grades, and portfolios in our study. No student included in the study will be identified by name. Mr. Morris and Mrs. Wheaton will assign code numbers to each student's academic record. These coded records will be followed while you're at Base Line Middle School to see how the Arts Focus Program affects achievement. Mr. Morris will keep the master code list in his possession in the building at all times so that no one will be able to see your grades and test scores.

We also would like to talk to you about your experiences in the Arts Focus Program and tape-record our conversation. The interview should take approximately 45 minutes to an hour, depending on how much you have to say. We will be tape-recording our conversation with you to ensure that we remember exactly what was said, but once we have completed the project, we will erase your tape. We will make sure no one, not even your teacher, sees or hears your interview, and we will use codes on the interviews instead of your name.

We do not believe that there are any risks to you if you participate in this project. However, we believe that your input will help improve the program. You may think about why you have been successful and/or frustrated in the program as you talk to us. You may also enjoy contributing to the improvement of the program.

Your participation in this study is voluntary, and you have the right to stop participating at any time. You also can refuse to answer any question(s) for any reason. In addition, we will use pseudonyms (cover names) to disguise the identity of all participants in any written or published material resulting from this study.

If you have any questions or concerns about participating in this project, or any unhappiness with any part of this study, you may talk to us or—confidentially—write to the Executive Secretary, Human Research Committee, Graduate School, Campus Box 26, Regent 308, University of Colorado, Boulder, CO 80309-0026, or call (303) 492-7401 and speak directly to the Executive Secretary.

Please sign both of these assent forms. The one on the back of this page is for you to keep, and the other is for our records. Please sign the next page and return it along with your parent's consent in the self-addressed envelope provided.

Assent Form for:

"Imagining the Future, Creating the Present: The Impact of Arts Education on Achievement and Identity in Arts Focus" (for students involved in the Arts Focus Program)

I understand the above information and agree to participate in the study titled "Imagining the Future, Creating the Present: The Impact of Arts Education on Achievement and Identity in Arts Focus."

Signature _____ *Date* _____

Please print your name _____

Please print the name of your parent(s) or guardian(s)

_____

APPENDIX C

Consent Form for a Life History Interview
(Ms. Maestas)

This interview was requested of an 86-year-old woman who had been a teacher and the wife of a teacher in New Mexico before its statehood. Mrs. Maestas knew the researcher because the researcher and her granddaughter were friends. Notwithstanding, Angela Johnson, the researcher, needed to obtain Mrs. Maestas's consent to participate in the study. Because of Mrs. Maestas's age, and because she had some difficulty in English, the letter had to be "translated" from the technical and academic language in which such letters are usually framed. Mrs. Maestas was very pleased to be asked to participate in this project. Furthermore, because she was very proud of her family's educational attainments, which reached well back into the 1800s, she wanted her own and their real names used.

October 15, 1996

Dear Mrs. Maestas;

I am a graduate student in education at the University of Colorado. I am doing a project for a class I'm taking at the University of Colorado on the history of schools in New Mexico. This class is being taught by Dr. Ruben Donato; his telephone number is 303-492-1000, and you can call him if you have any questions about the project.

I would be very interested in learning about your educational experiences in New Mexico and the education of your family. I would like your permission to tape record you when you tell me what you remember about going to school, what you learned, and what it was like to be a teacher. I will use the tapes of your interview to help me write my paper; after I'm done, I will return the tapes to you and your family, along with copies of the paper I write and transcripts of the tapes.

I am very excited about doing this project. Not many people realize that the Spanish American people in Northern New Mexico were graduating from high school and becoming teachers so long ago—even before the Anglo-Americans arrived from the East. I think it is very important that more people know your stories. If I do a good job on this paper, I hope to present it at conferences and maybe even submit it for publication in a journal or magazine for teachers and researchers in education.

If you would prefer, I can use a pseudonym or a fake name to protect your identity and the identity of your family members. If you have any more questions about this project or about the University of Colorado's policies about research on people, you can contact me at 417-2000 or Mary Ellen Ancell at the University of Colorado at 492-3000. Mrs. Ancell is the Executive Secretary of the Human Research Committee at the University of Colorado, which oversees all research projects involving people. You can report your concerns or ask your questions without fear that the Committee or Mrs. Ancell will tell anyone else that you called.

If you give your permission for me to interview you and to use the information in your interview for my paper, please read the statement of understanding below and sign on the line below it so I can show this form to the University.

Thank you for helping me.

Sincerely yours,

Angela Johnson

I understand the purpose of Angela Johnson's research project on the history of education in Northern New Mexico and I agree to be interviewed with a tape recorder for this project. I understand that I don't have to answer any questions that I don't feel like answering, and that I can end the interview any time that I wish.

Signed: _____

Date:: _____

APPENDIX D

Parental Consent in a Youth Community
Research Training Program

These consent forms were developed to ensure informed consent from parents and informed assent from young people in the Institute for Community Research's National Teen Action Research Center Summer Youth Research Institute. We wanted to make sure that parents knew that young people participating in the program were also going to be conducting research with their peers and participating in piloting research instruments on each other. The first form is filled out by parents, and the second by youth participants in the program. There is also a third form, not included here, which is meant to be filled out by parents of respondents in any surveys conducted by youth researchers. The procedures are consistent with the Institute for Community Research Institutional Review Board and with the requirements of the National Institute of Mental Health.

Consent Form
(parents of Institute participants)[4]

Minority Youth Action Research Training Institute is an after-school educational program being offered to Hartford-area youth between the ages of 15 and 18 during summers and throughout the school year. The summer program will provide employment to between 20 and 25 youth researchers to conduct youth risk-related research with their peers and to use the results for educational and intervention purposes. The yearlong program will provide participants with the opportunity to share their work in high schools and on college campuses in the Hartford and New Haven areas, learn about college careers, meet college students and faculty, and find related work for the remaining years of their high school career. Some students will be chosen to participate in a long-term evaluation of the program by interviewing their peers over a 3-year period about their experiences related to the program and to their career development and college plans. The topics to be discussed will be related to reproductive health, AIDS and drug risk, and violence. These topics have all been successfully researched by other teens in the past, and some of the results have been recognized with state and national awards.

Your child is being invited to join this program as a participant. Participants are expected to attend a 7-week action research training and implementation program during the summer. Each participant will be paid for his or her participation as a youth action researcher with summer youth employment money. In this program, participants will work with their peers and a team of supportive adults to identify a topic they want to study related to AIDS risk. They will then be helped to find ways of conducting the research with their team members. Then, they will be expected with their team to do the research with other young people in programs throughout the area, analyze the data, and decide how to use it for the benefit of their peers. Young researchers will receive special training in ensuring confidentiality and will be held accountable for their behavior consistent with this training at all times. During the summer period, they will meet with program adults on a regular basis to assess individual and group progress and experience in the program.

In order to record more accurately what is said, program adult staff may want to audio- or video-record sessions. The purpose of the taping will be to help youth record important discussions for their research purposes and to show how these taped data can be used for documentation purposes in a research project. The tapes will be kept in a locked file cabinet at the ICR office and will be transcribed without names or any form of other identification associated with the words transcribed. We will help youth to transcribe these tapes so that they can be used for research purposes related to the summer topic. No tapes will be used for external purposes without additional written consent from parents or caregivers and assent from youth themselves.

As part of the project, we will expect youth to attend four project meetings during the following school year and to work with team members to share the results of their work in their high school and on at least one college campus. We also expect participants to participate in at least four field trips to college campuses during the summer and during the school year. Participants will not receive compensation for the time put into these trips, but basic expenses (transportation and food) will be covered by the project.

At the end of the first year, we will help participants to find placements with other similar projects or faculty or adults working in the area of social science research in the Hartford area. All participants will also be asked to stay in touch with the program for 3 years and to participate in at least one brief interview each year for 3 years, with a project student and a staff member, to assess their experience with the program during that time and their progress since then. If your child is chosen as a student evaluator, he or she will become an employee of the ICR and will receive compensation for assisting with the longer-term evaluation of the project and the participants in it.

Your child's participation in this project is voluntary. However, once your child joins the project in the first year and accepts summer employment, we expect him or her to follow the guidelines for the project, which include regular attendance and performance, and to follow the personnel policies of the ICR, which will employ your child for the summer project and, if chosen, as a member of the student evaluation staff.

Confidentiality of Information: The organizations participating in this project are committed to ensuring the confidentiality of your child's responses to any evaluations that he or she participates in throughout the life of the program and to ensuring the anonymity of all information gathered in group discussions. Despite the commitment of all project staff and young people to maintain strict confidentiality of information, there is always a possible risk for loss of confidentiality. To protect participants from any possible risk, we will avoid the use of names at all times, and provide numerical codes for group discussions and unique identifiers for evaluation interviews. At no time during any group discussion will your child be asked to provide or to share personal information which he or she does not wish to share.

Benefits: Benefits of participation include 1 year of summer employment in the program, learning how to conduct applied social science research, assistance with school career and school work, introduction to college campuses and contacts, and potential for employment in the future.

Risks and Discomforts: Drug prevention research and program preparation may involve topics that relate to your child's personal concerns about risk, behaviors, and lifestyle. Discussion of these issues—either by your child or by others—may cause your child to experience emotional distress. If he or she feels this way, your child will be able to talk with any of the project facilitators about his or her feelings if he or she wishes. Some participants may feel social pressure from their peers to participate or to not participate. Participants may be concerned about their peers' and group members' respect for confidentiality of response in group discussions.

Research Questions: If you have *questions about the research* in this project, you may contact Jean J. Schensul, project principal investigator (860) 278-2044, ext. 227, or Sandra Sydlo, project director, at (860) 278-2044, ext. 273. Or, if you have any *questions about your rights as a project participant or to research-related injuries,* you may contact Henrietta Bernal at (860) 679-1570.

Termination: Circumstances under which your child's participation may be terminated by an administrative staff person without regard to your consent include disruptive or unruly behavior or consistent inability to perform in a manner that meets the standards of the program, which will be explained to you and your child when your child joins the project.

I HEREBY CERTIFY THAT I HAVE READ THIS CONSENT FORM OR HAD IT READ TO ME, I UNDERSTAND ITS CONTENT, AND AGREE TO PARTICIPATE IN THIS PROJECT, INCLUDING THE AUDIOTAPING OF GROUP SESSIONS.

_____

Print Name

_____   _____

Signature of Assenting Youth   *Date*

_____   _____

Interviewer Name   *Date*

---

4. This consent form will be presented through discussion and explanation in detail, as well as in written form, with each participant to ensure comprehension and agreement using procedures for checking outlined in the grant application.

Assent Form (for programs)[5]

Minority Youth Action Research Training Institute is an after-school educational program being offered to Hartford-area youth between the ages of 15 and 18 during summers and throughout the school year. The summer program will provide employment to between 20 and 25 youth researchers to conduct youth risk-related research with their peers and to use the results for educational and intervention purposes. The yearlong program will provide participants with the opportunity to share their work in high schools and on college campuses in the Hartford and New Haven areas, learn about college careers, meet college students and faculty, and find related work for the remaining years of their high school career. Some students will be chosen to participate in a long-term evaluation of the program by interviewing their peers over a 3-year period about their experiences related to the program and to their career development and college plans. The topics to be discussed will be related to reproductive health, AIDS and drug risk, and violence. These topics have all been successfully researched by other teens in the past, and some of the results have been recognized with state and national awards.

The summer program in which you are a participant is one of 10 or more summer programs that are being invited to help young researchers in this program by involving youth in providing anonymous data for the use of these young researchers. This means that youth researchers will make two visits to the program during the summer. The first will be to explain the project they are conducting and to ask youth to participate in a group data collection exercise. The second will be to provide some preliminary results of their research to all of the groups who participated, and to discuss the issue in a health education format.

At all times during these two sessions, you will be accompanied by trained ICR adult program staff and by the adult staff of your summer program.

Your agreement to participate in this project is voluntary. If you choose to be uninvolved in the program sessions, your supervisor or youth worker will provide you with another activity during the time that youth researchers are working with other children in your group. There will be no penalty or any other negative consequence associated with your decision to be involved in another activity at this time, except that you might wish to be with your friends rather than in another activity.

Confidentiality of Information: The organizations participating in this project are committed to ensuring the confidentiality of children's responses to group questions or other information collection. Everything you say will be kept absolutely confidential, except when program staff judge that your personal safety is in danger. In such a case, we are subject to the laws of the state with regard to the protection of youth and children. Despite the commitment of all project staff and young people to maintain strict confidentiality of information, there is always a possible risk for loss of confidentiality. To protect participants from any possible risk, we will ensure the confidentiality of all information gathered in group discussions by avoiding the use of names at all times when individual data sheets are collected and by providing numerical codes for group discussions. At no time during any group discussion will you be asked to provide or share personal information about your own or your family's involvement in risk behavior or be pressed to provide any other information that you do not wish to share. Young researchers will receive special training in ensuring confidentiality and will be held accountable for their behavior with regard to confidentiality at all times.

Benefits: Benefits of participation include the opportunity to observe other young people in training for careers, engage in a peer education experience, think about critical issues in AIDS or other risk prevention that are developmentally appropriate, and access the training program in the future.

Risks and Discomforts: Participation in the discussions may involve topics that relate to your personal concerns about your own risk, behaviors, and lifestyle. Discussion of these issues may cause you to experience some emotional distress. If you feel this way, you will be able to talk with summer program staff or any of the adult project facilitators at any time. Some participants may feel social pressure from their peers to participate or not to participate. Participants may be concerned about their peers' and group members' respect for confidentiality of response in group discussions.

Research Questions: If you have *questions about the research* in this project, you may contact Jean J. Schensul, project principal investigator (860) 278-2044, ext. 227, or Sandra Sydlo, project director, at (860) 278-2044, ext. 273. Or, if you have any *questions about your rights as a project participant or to research-related injuries,* you may contact Henrietta Bernal at (860) 679-1570.

Termination: Circumstances under which your participation may be terminated by an administrative staff person without regard to your consent include disruptive or unruly behavior or consistent inability to perform in a manner that meets the standards of the program, which will be explained to you in the session.

I HEREBY CERTIFY THAT I HAVE READ THIS CONSENT FORM OR HAD IT READ TO ME, I UNDERSTAND ITS CONTENT, AND AGREE TO PARTICIPATE IN THIS PROJECT, INCLUDING THE AUDIOTAPING OF GROUP SESSIONS.

_____

Print Name

_____   _____

Signature of Assenting Youth   *Date*

_____   _____

Interviewer Name   *Date*

---

5. This consent form will be presented through discussion and explanation in detail, as well as in written form, with each participant to ensure comprehension and agreement using procedures for checking outlined in the grant application.

—

2

BUILDING RESEARCH
PARTNERSHIPS

JEAN J. SCHENSUL
MARGARET WEEKS
MERRILL SINGER

We begin this chapter by describing different types of **research partnerships** involving ethnographers, other researchers, and nonresearcher partners. A research partnership involves an equitable collaboration between ethnographers, researchers from other disciplines, or non-researchers to address a common research problem. Research partnerships are relatively new. The first section of this chapter discusses some of the factors, such as the introduction of new technology and community interest in research and results, that have contributed to the formation of research collaborations. Ethnographers may choose among several different types of partnerships. For example, they may work in local, national, or even cross-national ethnographic teams. Or, they may become members of interdisciplinary research teams. More recently, ethnographers have begun to work collaboratively with service and program partners or policymakers and advocates to bring about changes in community life. Most of the remainder of the chapter is devoted to a discussion of each of these three types of partnerships. We define the type of partnerships,

Definition:
A research partnership involves an equitable collaboration between ethnographers, researchers from other disciplines, or nonresearchers around a common research problem

85

give examples of such partnerships, and describe problems that can arise in the field, methodological and ethical considerations, strengths and limitations of the partnership type, and provide a checklist that allows readers to assess congruence between partnership needs and individual interests and motivations.

Ethnographers have always recognized the importance of people who have helped them to gain access to communities, key sources of information, and their own families and personal networks. There is a substantial literature in anthropology and sociology devoted to entry into the field and the importance of building relationships with helpful and knowledgeable people (cf. Bernard, 1995; Boas, 1948; Wolcott, 1995). When entering the field, ethnographers have sought out people of like mind who can help them gain access to the people, places, and information they need to answer their research questions. As we said in Chapter 1 of this book, we cannot manage without these partners, whom we term key informants or gatekeepers. They become friends and colleagues—people with whom we can exchange ideas, and partners in the data collection and interpretation process. They are so important to fieldwork that Oswald Werner and Mark Schoepfle have referred to them as "consultants" (Werner & Schoepfle, 1987a, 1987b). *Many of the ethical dilemmas that arise in the course of ethnographic field research stem from the deep and personal relationships that ethnographic researchers establish with their key informants.* These relationships—so important for the research process—may result in contradictions between the needs and requests of key informants and ethical principles and demands of the research endeavor.

Nevertheless, despite their importance to researchers, key informants historically have not been viewed as research partners, nor have they been seen as central in shaping the research agenda or involved in the analysis of data. Ethnographers have been trained to think of themselves as

Cross Reference:
See Book 2, Chapter 4 on entering the field

Key point with Cross Reference:
See Chapter 1, this volume, on the role of the researcher

the single instrument of data collection, analysis, and presentation. They identify their topic, apply their methods, collect their fieldnotes and other qualitative (or quantitative) data, and write them up. Going to the field alone (or with a partner or family members) has long been a rite of passage for ethnographers. Anthropologists like to tell stories of "the time when I was dropped on the main street of a town in northern Minnesota and left there"; or "When I arrived in Tacit, Sinhaloa, and couldn't speak a word of Spanish"; or "When they unlocked the front door of the school and I walked down the hall to the principal's office for the first time, I knew I was on my own." Being alone and lonely in the field is a common refrain in anthropological field diaries, and loneliness is a significant element in culture shock.

Research field schools and professor-student teamwork in the field are traditional ways of training students to conduct ethnography. However, participation in ethnographic or interdisciplinary research teams, working in equivalent pairs or larger teams with nonresearchers, or building networks of organizations to engage in participatory or collaborative research have only recently become part of the ethnographer's repertoire. There are few examples of interdisciplinary projects in which ethnographic researchers have participated as equals. Two historically important exceptions are the Vicos Project, which involved anthropologists as well as other social science researchers from Cornell in the research and redevelopment of the Hacienda known as Vicos in highland Peru (Holmberg, 1954, 1958, 1966), and the Six Cultures study, in which ethnographers addressed socialization practices in six countries (Whiting & Whiting, 1975)

In the 1980s, collections by Eddy and Partridge (1987), Schensul and Eddy (1985), Schensul and Stern (1985), and Stull and Schensul (1987) summarized examples of collaborative or team ethnographic and interdisciplinary research experiences in the United States and elsewhere. Newer publications by Reason (1988), Whyte (1991), Scrimshaw and Gleason (1992), Schensul and Schensul (1992), Bartunek and Louis (1996), and Erickson and Stull (1998) illustrate a variety of different approaches to conducting ethnographically driven team research for community development and program enhancement. These experiences offer models for the development of research partnerships that improve both the quality and the utility of ethnographic research.

ENVIRONMENTAL CHANGES
FAVORING PARTNERSHIPS

Factors Favoring Research Partnerships

- Complex social problems that require interdisciplinary approaches
- Improvements in ethnographic research technology resulting in more rigorous field research methods and tools
- Changes in perceptions of the right to representation favoring active community participation
- Changes in communications technology making within- and cross-site communication easier

A number of changes have occurred over the past 30 years to make real research partnership both necessary and feasible. Some are technological and methodological. Others involve transformations in the knowledge base of communities and other institutions where ethnography traditionally has been carried out. These changes in literacy, education level, access to electronic communication, and political awareness have enabled communities to begin to define their own research needs and to call upon researchers for assistance.

Solving Complex Social Problems
Requires Interdisciplinary Approaches

Ethnographers interested in applying their work to solving social problems recognize that most social issues are complex. Working on the problem requires both the participation of the communities or institutions experiencing the problem and the involvement of scientists from different disciplines and traditions. Studying learning problems in children, for instance, may call for ethnographic observation of children learning in particular social contexts, a psychologically based understanding of how learning occurs, a formal assessment by school psychologists using culturally appropriate tools, and physicians to determine the potential impact of clinical health problems on learning. The increasing emphasis on improving service or instructional quality and the search for process as well as outcome evaluation has thrust ethnographers into new arrangements with epidemiologists, psychologists, and other social and biological scientists in order to answer service providers' questions.

Improvements in Ethnographic
Research Methodology and Technology

There is now a large body of literature on ethnographic research methods, and there are many training opportunities for ethnographers who wish to gain instruction and practice in conducting ethnographic research. Certainly, it is still possible to find social science students who have not received training in research methods. Nevertheless, today, no one need be in the position of going to the field without guidelines for entry, basic and enhanced data collection methods, and recording and analysis skills. The **Ethnographer's Toolkit** is one of a series of publications available to help prospective field researchers define in advance every step in an ethnographic field study (cf. Bernard, 1995, 1998;

Crabtree & Miller, 1992; Denzin & Lincoln, 1994; Le-Compte, Millroy, & Preissle, 1992; LeCompte & Preissle, 1993; Pelto & Pelto, 1978; Werner & Schoepfle, 1987a, b). Summer methods schools or "camps" are now available in many locations in the United States and elsewhere. We have a common language and set of methods for defining research questions and for sampling, collecting, coding, analyzing, and writing up qualitative data. Computer-based data management packages help with the tedious process of coding, managing, and analyzing large bodies of ethnographic text data, such as field observations of behavior or social settings and conversations with informants (Lee & Fielding, 1996; Miles & Huberman, 1994). These technological tools require ethnographers to define and operationalize their variables clearly and early on in the data collection process in order to communicate with one another and with the software designed to help them do so. Computer programs make it easier for teams of ethnographers to define commonalities across settings and sites and to analyze their data together.

Cross Reference: See Book 5, Chapter 6, on electronic management and analysis of text data

Changes in Perceptions of the Right to Representation

Cross Reference: The issue of representation is discussed in greater detail in Book 1, Chapter 3, and Book 7, Chapter 1

There have been continuing discussions regarding representation, or who has the right to portray the culture or lifestyle of the group in question and the ways in which it is portrayed. In the past, ethnographers' views and descriptions were rarely challenged by either colleagues or key informants. Only occasionally did two ethnographers separately enter the same field to investigate the same phenomenon. When they did, it was usually at two different time points, making it impossible to disaggregate the effects of time and history from the separate interpretations of the ethnographers themselves (Freeman, 1983; Lewis, 1966; Redfield, 1941). Furthermore, most of the people in the communities described by ethnographers were not literate, and key informants could not read materials written about them. Thus, they were not in a position to discuss or debate the research findings (cf. Clifford & Marcus, 1986).

Now, the communities that ethnographers study are increasingly literate. Community leaders, educational administrators, and target populations—participants in research ventures—are also increasingly politicized (Brosted et al., 1985; Greaves, 1994; Manderson, Kelaher, Williams, & Shannon, 1998; Whyte, 1991). They have learned that they have the right to question, and that research, if conducted properly, can work to their advantage. They also have something to say about how best to carry out the research because they know their constituents better than the researchers do. The Internet offers communities from one end of the globe to the other the power of instant communication and access to information never before available. It is not surprising, then, that although ethnographers seek research partners, at the same time community constituencies more and more often seek researchers to help them answer pressing questions related to improving their quality of life or their ability to advocate for themselves and for others.

Accessing research communities—including clinics and schools—requires that researchers demonstrate the utility of their research. An important component in demonstrating utility is involving potential critics and users in the research process. *If research is a powerful tool for influencing policy and public opinion, then communities should have influence over what kind of research is conducted, and whether or not the tools of research used in each setting are appropriate.*

Key point

Changes in Communications Technology
Improve Research Communication

In the past, prior to the use of computers and the immediacy of electronic mail, conducting field research on the same topic using the same methodological approaches in different communities or different countries was difficult and costly. Working out the details of research design, sampling, and questionnaire design were best done face to face, requiring high transportation costs. Problems identified in a field site waited for mail responses, which could take a month or more. Batches of data—text or numerical—were handwritten or typed and sent by regular mail, sometimes resulting in lengthy delays. Now face-to-face communication via teleconferencing is possible, at least in Western countries. E-mail and wireless electronic communication are available in most locations throughout the world, making cross-site and cross-national ethnographic research more convenient and cost-effective.

To sum up, the methods and tools of ethnography, coupled with electronic communication, now make it more possible, feasible, and cost-effective for ethnographers in the field to communicate with one another across sites, across regional locations, and even globally. At the same time, improved literacy and the spread of telecommunications technology have changed the social environment of research and promoted greater balance in the relationship between researchers and the community of study. It behooves ethnographers, then, to know more about how to build good partnering relationships for the benefit of better research and better use of their research results.

Working in partnerships is exciting and challenging. Partners open doors to communities, to experience, to the creation of new research methods, and to new ways of interpreting research results. Partnerships also introduce new challenges into the field experience and call for new social as well as intellectual skills in order to make sure that communication goes smoothly and that the views of all partners are considered in the negotiation of a study and its uses. Finally, partnerships may have their downside. For example, they can call into question the authority of ethnographers as social scientists to state their views, especially when those views are not popular or display community dynamics in a less than positive light. The remainder of this chapter is intended to help researchers consider the advantages of as well as the difficulties and potential challenges in building different types of research partnerships.

TYPES OF ETHNOGRAPHIC RESEARCH PARTNERSHIPS

Partnerships for Ethnographic Research

■ Ethnographic research teams where ethnographers are engaged in common-site or cross-site research and pool their data in a common database.

■ Interdisciplinary research teams composed of representatives from different disciplines, in which ethnographers may either direct/manage the research or a component of a larger study or participate as ethnographers on the team

■ Action research teams composed of ethnographers who work as members of a larger team of both researchers and interventionists (such as teachers, farmers, community developers, health educators, and community activists) and who want to conduct research to solve a pressing social problem

Ethnographic research partnerships can take many forms. *The most important criterion for definition of a partnership is that at least two people—one of whom must be an ethnographic researcher—are engaged in the research together.* Engagement means some degree of involvement in all of the steps of a research project as outlined in Book 1,

Key point

Cross Reference:
See Book 1,
Chapters 4 and 5,
on research design
and choosing and
designing an
ethnographic
research project

Chapters 4 and 5, from defining the problem through collecting, analyzing, presenting, and using the data. Ethnographers can partner with others in the conduct of ethnographic, as well as survey, network, experimental, and other forms of research in all of the ways listed above. Each of the three research partnerships mentioned on the previous page involves ethnographers in different kinds of relationships and requires somewhat different types of skills and responsibilities.

BUILDING ETHNOGRAPHIC RESEARCH TEAMS

What Is an Ethnographic Research Team?

Definition:
An ethnographic research
team includes two or
more ethnographers
studying the same
topic together

An **ethnographic research team** consists of two or more ethnographers who are studying the same topic together using ethnographic methods. Joint studies can occur in the same field site (common-site), or in geographically separated field sites selected for comparability (multisite).

Ethnography is primarily inductive—that is, it usually begins with a very general framework and set of exploratory questions. The key to the ethnographic team venture is coming to agreement on a common set of issues, approaches, and concepts to be addressed in the study that have validity for each ethnographer and for each site in a multisite study. Some refer to this process as a perpetual dialogue—a continuous process of negotiation that must be tended if it is to be successful.

The challenge of perpetual dialogue to team ethnography can be met best if field team members get together regularly to discuss conceptual matters, compare data collection strategies, evolve coding systems, and conduct ongoing data analysis. As we pointed out earlier, some aspects of this process now can be facilitated at a distance with electronic communication. However, even when ethnographers hold the topic of the research to be of great impor-

tance and can meet face to face, cultural and social differences between field sites and differences among ethnographers in training, experience, and theoretical perspective
can compound the challenges of working together. *Thus,*   **Key point**
discussion, dialogue, self-reflection, and careful communi-
cations facilitation on the part of the team leader are all
critical ingredients in team ethnography.

Examples of Ethnographic Teamwork

There are some examples of ethnographic teamwork in
the literature. Pertti Pelto's team fieldwork in both northern
Minnesota and central Mexico (Pelto & Pelto, 1978) are
classic examples of the teacher and advanced student team
approach in the field. The summer and year-round field
study programs described by Simon, Simonelli, and Ervin
(1998) in workshops at the 1998 Society for Applied Anthropology meetings, or those implemented by the University of Chicago's Department of Sociology under the direction of William Julius Wilson, are examples of the field
school model of ethnographic team research which involve
students. Below, we discuss several examples of ethnographic teamwork in which the ethnographers are not students but are fully developed professionals with advanced
degrees who are central figures in each study.

➤•➤•➤   **EXAMPLE 2.1**

BUILDING AN ETHNOGRAPHIC FIELD TEAM IN A SINGLE SITE

In 1988, the Institute for Community Research and the Hispanic Health Council
embarked on a long-term partnership to study AIDS risk behaviors in injection drug
users, crack cocaine users, and their sex partners, and to use the research results to
improve preventive interventions. The first studies, guided by a combination of street
outreach, educational interventions, and epidemiologic panel studies, recruited approximately 10% of injection drug users in the city of Hartford and elsewhere in the
country with generally positive outcomes.

Eventually, it became clear that street outreach was able to attract only a small percentage of the total drug-using population in any given city (Singer, Irizarry, & Schensul, 1991). New approaches were needed. As a result, the Institute for Community Research and the Hispanic Health Council decided to investigate the potential in the community for mobilizing specific settings and designated social roles for risk prevention. This has entailed the development of ethnographic study of drug risk settings, high-risk site/shooting gallery **gatekeepers**, violence, AIDS and drugs, and patterns of initiation of injection drug use. Six funded studies, each of which includes ethnographic components, are now in the field. Ethnographers Singer, Weeks, and Schensul are principal investigators or co-investigators for these studies, and the studies are staffed by teams of ethnographers and outreach experts who know the target communities. Although the specific research problems funded and addressed by each study are somewhat different, ethnographic and network methods are similar. Ethnographic research teams meet separately by project to discuss field research problems and strategies; they also meet together across projects to discuss common issues and themes.

 Definition: Gatekeepers are those who control access to the site and may sell drugs to those who use the site

Conceptualization, coding, instrument development, and management of ethical and practical issues in the field have undergone protracted discussion, joint training sessions, and the development of guidelines including the do's and don'ts of fieldwork among active drug users. Investigators have concluded that an important component of all of the studies is a text-based coding system. The coding system evolved through the interaction of experienced ethnographers, outreach workers, and the field data, and the system has been tested in the field. The cross-site team of ethnographers (and ethnographic outreach workers) has come to an agreement about major codes (domain codes) that will be used to code all text-based data, regardless of project. Ethnographic researchers affiliated with specific studies will use subdomains and finer units related to specific study foci. The development of the joint coding system, although not without its conflicts and healthy disagreements, has affirmed commonality of interests across projects, built commitment across partner organizations, and helped to solve problems in the field.

━•━•━•━

The next example describes a project in which ethnographers simultaneously studied school reform in not one but nine locations across the United States.

DOING CROSS-SITE SCHOOL ETHNOGRAPHY

The Center for New Schools in Chicago, an education-oriented research, training, and technical assistance organization, received a contract to study educational innovations in nine locations across the country using ethnographic methods. Each site was already recognized for its ability to bring about positive educational results; the sites also represented a broad range of cultural experience and ethnic and racial diversity. The challenges to the research team were two: First, to discover what the innovations really were, how the process of innovation in administration and classroom instruction was happening in schools, and the relationship of these changes to local communities; and second, to extract the best lessons from all nine sites to use in the creation and evaluation of educational innovations in two new demonstration sites.

Ethnographers were hired in each of the nine sites. They were chosen because of their prior experience in conducting ethnographic research in schools and their ethnic match with the primary student body in each educational setting. A sociologist with a background in ethnographic evaluation was hired by the contracting organization to develop an observational scheme with the researchers at each of the sites. The scheme was designed to capture the range of topics believed to be important in educational innovation across sites. This process, which combined face-to-face site visits, feedback by mail and telephone conferencing from the central site to the field, and joint meetings of all of the field researchers in one of two central locations—Chicago or New York—resulted in a final observational and coding system.

Researchers conducted their observations and sent in coded fieldnotes on a monthly basis. Fieldnotes were reviewed for coding accuracy, stored, and hand searched, because desktop computers and computerized text-based data management programs were not available at that time. Such procedures still can be used where electronic equipment is not readily available. The data management and analysis process resulted in site-specific ethnographies as well as a cross-site report

Cross Reference: See Book 5, Chapters 4 and 5, on coding text data

that reflected an analysis of comparable units, patterns, and structures across the sites. The cross-site report was possible only because coding categories had been agreed upon beforehand.

The following situation describes an arrangement for conducting team research that reaches across continents.

EXAMPLE 2.3

CONDUCTING ETHNOGRAPHIC RESEARCH ACROSS CONTINENTS

The year 1983 marked the beginning of a long-term program of research, training, and intervention exchange between the University of Connecticut and the University of Peradeniya (Sri Lanka). Later, the team grew to include the University of Antwerp, the Institute for Community Research in Hartford, and State University of New York—Albany (SUNYA). In 1987, to facilitate joint studies, medical and social sciences faculty members at the University of Peradeniya established an independent nonprofit research center—The Center for Intersectoral Community Health Studies—in the city of Kandy, a provincial capital just east of the university. The Kandy-based nongovernmental organization (NGO) is staffed by ethnographers (mainly anthropologists and sociologists) and their students.

From 1994 to 1997, a study funded through the Washington, D.C.-based International Center for Research on Women addressed the issue of sexuality and HIV risk in youth and young adults in the Kandy area and at the university. The study design developed by investigators from both countries called for participant observation, in-depth and semistructured interviewing, and an ethnographic survey. Investigators from both countries met several times in Sri Lanka at strategic points in the conduct of the research to do the following:

Cross Reference: See Book 2, Chapter 3, for a discussion of how theory informs plans for research

- Develop coding trees
- Plan for in-depth and semistructured interviews and observations
- Create and pilot the ethnographic survey and train field interviewers
- Revise the survey schedule
- Enter, clean, and analyze data

A 1-month residency for the entire field team of ethnographers at the Rockefeller Conference Center in Bellagio, Italy, allowed 11 co-investigators time to complete data analysis together and to write the first draft of a monograph on youth and sexual risk in Sri Lanka (Silva et al., 1997). The results of the research were disseminated nationally to representatives of the Ministries of Health and Women's Affairs, and to nongovernmental organizations across the country. Joint rules for publication allow investigators from either country to publish articles based on study data after consultation with the principal investigator(s) in each country. Papers and monographs are multiple-authored. Two main factors have contributed to the success of this international research exchange: The commitment and ability of the senior researchers to work together across continents, and their ability to generate continuous funding for work in Sri Lanka.

Developing and Maintaining Ethnographic Research Teams

These examples suggest that a strong ethnographic research team rests on the following foundation:

- Competent and committed ethnographers willing to work as team members
- Participatory training in the fundamentals of the study
- Clear roles and responsibilities
- Good communication
- Team participation in the development of conceptualization, data collection, coding, and analysis procedures
- Resolution of issues of ownership of data and results and access to the same

Hiring and Training Team Ethnographers

Finding experienced ethnographers who are both interested in the topic of study and a good match for the target population is a challenging task. "Ethnographer" is still not a recognized job category. However, developing a good job description and posting the search in regional departments of sociology and anthropology; advertising in publications read by social scientists, such as the *Chronicle of Higher Education*; using professional organizations' web sites and newsletters; and listing on the Internet usually produces a number of appropriate candidates. Criteria for hiring for team projects should include prior experience as a member of an ethnographic research team (or, at minimum, working in some capacity in a team fieldwork context). In addition, ethnographers working in a team context should demonstrate willingness to share information and contacts, distribute their coded fieldnotes, and share data with other team members for research development and publication purposes. *Candidates who are enthusiastic about sharing and discussing their ethnographic data and insights will make good team colleagues and associates.*

Cross Reference: Book 1, Chapter 8 on who should do ethnographic research

Key point

Participatory Training in the Study's Fundamentals

Training an ethnographic field team is an ongoing activity. Members of the team may not have equivalent prior training: For example, some may have experience only in participant observation and in-depth interviewing; others may also have experience with semistructured interviewing, network research, or elicitation techniques. On-the-job training equalizes the balance of skills on the team.

The skills of ethnographic field team members should complement one another. Team members with different skills can train each other in the use of different approaches to data collection. Often, one member of a team will show leadership in a specific area of ethnographic research. For example, in the study mentioned in Example 2.5 on drug users' use of high-risk sites, when the data analyst familiar with NUD*IST, a text-based data management program, left the project for another position, one of the ethnographers took over the responsibility of setting up the text coding system, updating it, and entering it into NUD·IST so that other ethnographers could concentrate on data collection and coding.

All staff members in a team project need to be familiarized with the design and theoretical background of the study at the start of the project. Further conceptual training occurs as the team is involved in developing and testing the project's text coding system. Finally, specialized training in such areas as network analysis, electronic data entry, use of computers in the field, and sampling methodology should be considered and consultants in these areas introduced as necessary.

Roles and Responsibilities

As in any team endeavor, one of the main challenges in managing an ethnographic field team is creating a clear definition of team roles and responsibilities. A typical team structure is the following:

- *Principal investigator (team leader/project director):* leads the team that writes the research grant, is responsible to the funder for technical and financial aspects of the work and reporting, directs the conceptual work, and organizes the work domains of the rest of the team
- *Project coordinator:* responsible for day-to-day management of the work flow as well as some field research and data organizing and management tasks
- *Team ethnographers/researchers:* responsible for specific domains of research as designated through dialogue with the team leader and project coordinator and generally defined by both the project and the ethnographer, who may favor specific domains of investigation arising from the fieldwork
- *Data analyst:* responsible for helping to formulate the development of an ethnographic survey, creating data management systems for quantitative data, and assisting with the interface or triangulation of qualitative and quantitative data
- *Project outreach workers/students:* assist in observations, interviews, locating key informants and survey respondents, searching for literature, coding, and other project tasks

■ *Project support staff:* Provide general secretarial and management support to research activities

The domains of responsibility represented by these staffing categories are important in any project, regardless of whether it is a large, nationally funded study; an ethnographic field team; or one person's dissertation research assisted by part-time data collectors in the field.

EXAMPLE 2.4   ━●━●━●━

AN ETHNOGRAPHIC STUDY OF PARENT INVOLVEMENT
IN SPECIAL EDUCATION PLACEMENT

Anthropologist Pertti Pelto received a contract from a federal funding source to conduct an ethnographic study of the way decisions were being made about the placement of children in special education programs in a Connecticut elementary school. The purpose of the study was to discover and describe the role of parents in the decision-making process under U.S. Public Law 94142, which called for parental involvement in placement decisions. The study team consisted of the lead investigator, Dr. Pelto; a project coordinator/ethnographer, Dr. Jean Schensul; two part-time ethnographers; and a student administrator. The lead investigator guided the research, generated the research design, monitored work in the field, headed field team meetings, and wrote the final report and publications. The project coordinator was responsible for data collection and coordination of the work of each of the part-time students, including feedback on fieldnotes. She also wrote first drafts of reports. The ethnographers were assigned to specific domains of observation and interviewing in the school, as well as interviewing a sample of parents. The administrator kept all fieldnotes and took detailed ethnographic minutes at meetings that were added to the database and were tracked for project decision making (Yoshida, Schensul, & Pelto, 1978).

━●━●━●━

Clear division of labor and delineation of responsibilities is even more critical for a research team whose members, working in the same setting, are expected to gather similar or complementary data. Guided by the team leader (usually the principal investigator or technical team leader), members of the team should know the following:

Key point

- Which data they should be collecting and in what periods of time
- In what forms the data are to be recorded
- When regular meetings to discuss findings will be held
- What they are expected to prepare for these meetings
- Where they are expected to conduct their research
- When reports and other written materials are due

Guidelines for the work should be recorded in writing to avoid confusion. Ideally, work schedules, responsibilities, and areas of data collection should evolve in guided discussions among field team members rather than being imposed by the team leader. Field researchers working in the same field setting at the same time must pay special attention to these requirements so that they do not duplicate information collection unnecessarily, or unknowingly use the same key informants.

In same-site ethnographic team research, team members may develop overlapping sets of key informants. As we noted in Chapter 1 of this book, the traditional relationship between ethnographers and key informants is one of personal attachment and reciprocal commitment. Both the friendship and the source of information become valuable. It is certainly possible, especially in small towns and cities, that key informants can offer different types of information to different people in the same project at different times. Therefore, it is important to discuss the overlap in relation-

Cross Reference: See Chapter 1 of this book, and Book 2, Chapter 4, on relationships between ethnographers and key informants

ships. One option is to introduce the individual to the entire project in order to avoid conflict among team members and confusion about the project on the part of the key informant. A second is to clarify for the key informant the names, purposes, and organization of the projects and which fieldworkers are involved in them.

Research team meetings should be recorded ethnographically, that is, a recorder should be assigned to each meeting to record the decisions made regarding next steps, as well as the content of the discussion. It is especially important to record field team meetings because it is here that some of the first steps in analysis are made as team members share their observations for the week or the month. The recorder should be someone who is not running the meeting, if possible, although rotating responsibility for recording is a way of avoiding recording burnout. In a study of drug-use transitions at the Institute for Community Research, for example, all full-time research staff, including the Principal Investigator, rotate the recording of team meeting notes. The meeting notes should be distributed immediately to each team member and amplified in order to make sure that history is captured accurately and that all ideas are recorded. Notes of team meetings should be included for coding in the ethnographic text database.

Cultural units and patterns (the building blocks for structures or qualitative hypothesis development and testing) appear in fieldnotes, but a perceptive team leader will discover them far more quickly by listening carefully in ethnographic team meetings while ethnographers are discussing their findings for the week or month. Team decisions can then be made with respect to new research directions, as the following vignette illustrates.

➤•➤•➤   **EXAMPLE 2.5**

REDEFINING THE TERM *HIGH-RISK SITES* IN A HARTFORD DRUG STUDY

During a period of exploratory ethnography, a team of two ethnographers paired with two field outreach workers collected data on the locations that heroin and cocaine injectors and crack smokers go to use drugs in the city. In the process of tracking these locations through interviewing and observation, this team of field researchers docu-

mented frequent use of abandoned buildings for rapid "get-off." These locations were often extremely dilapidated and uninviting, but they offered shelter, hiding, and access without having to gain entry through a gatekeeper. Experienced outreach workers noted that the use of abandoned buildings for

Definition:
"Get-off" is a
street term for
injecting drugs
to get high

this purpose had increased over the use of enclosed, gatekeeper-controlled spaces, which had been common even 5 years earlier. This transition, documented by all members of the team, led the researchers to reconceptualize their definition of high-risk sites and retarget their research to balance open sites and inside sites for study and potential intervention.

➤•➤•➤

Communication

Maintaining good communication among members of a field team is very important. Team members depend on one another for shared information and the identification of new challenges in the field setting. Good communication produces the important insights called for in ethnographic research. When team members notice new patterns in the data they are collecting, they may share their observations with their team members well before formal meeting times. This can produce better and more focused observation or interviewing. Good communication can also protect a field team and the organization in which it is based. For example, one field worker may discover that inaccurate rumors regarding the intentions of a field study are spreading in the community. Reporting this immediately to the rest of the team can help to address the problem before it affects the well-being of the project.

Despite our emphasis on teamwork, there are individualistic aspects of team ethnography. Researchers must count on their own styles and their interviewing and observational skills and abilities to enter a research setting and successfully obtain useful information for the study. Researchers often use different strategies in the field. For example, some researchers are more outgoing; others prefer to listen unobtrusively for a long time. Some enjoy group encounters and informal group conversations; others are more effective one-on-one. One team member may have more experience in the study community than another or may match the study population characteristics more closely, making initial access easier. ***Team leaders must assess the strengths of the field team and assist team members to complement each others' skills and abilities in order to prevent intrateam competition and ensure maximum productivity.***

Key point

Despite their different responsibilities, team members should expect to produce work at approximately the same rate. Nothing is more discouraging to team spirit than unequal production. Team members should be clear about how productivity is measured and should be assisted to produce steadily and at a standardized rate.

Trust among team members is necessary for free-flowing communication to occur. Trust among team members is built when:

- Communication is open.
- Team roles and responsibilities are clear and well understood.
- Responsibility for team problems and successes is shared.
- Rules for ensuring staff confidentiality are clear and enforced
- Workloads are fairly distributed.
- Job assignments, deadlines, and work schedules are unambiguous.
- Procedures for conflict resolution, raising of issues, and expression of grievances are clear.
- Team members feel intellectually and emotionally safe in their work.
- Every team member who desires to do so has an opportunity to take the lead on publications.
- Publications are multiply authored.
- Rules for publication are jointly developed, clear, and followed.
- Personal as well as project ambitions are respected and balanced (Erickson & Stull, 1998).

Finally, clear roles and responsibilities and guidelines for individual as well as group achievement help to avoid competition and to advance interdependence.

Producing, Managing, Coding, and Analyzing Text Data in Team Ethnography

Nothing is more important for furthering the work of an ethnographic field team than the steady production of fieldnotes. *Fieldnotes are the trademark of good ethnography, and regular writing of fieldnotes should be encouraged for all ethnographers in a team situation.* Care in notetaking is always desirable, but it is especially important when an ethnographer is alone in the field and, at the same time, is responsible for reporting to a group.

Key point

Ethnographers recognize that the immediacy of experience is important in ethnographic field research. One of the purposes of well-written fieldnotes is to recreate the immediacy of the interview or observed event so that other members of the team can relive it. Good fieldnotes need not read as well as a good piece of fiction, but they should provide enough details so that new readers (i.e., team members) can reconstruct an event or interview.

Ethnographers working in teams must record their notes as quickly as possible and make them accessible to other team members in order to ensure effective information sharing. These notes and discussions about them provide an opportunity for every member of the team, including the team leader, to gain a comprehensive picture of the field situation. Team leaders must be persistent in encouraging ethnographic team members to produce their fieldnotes regularly and quickly so that all team members can access them in an expedient manner.

Cross Reference: See Book 1, Chapter 8, on who should do ethnography

If you are considering joining an ethnographic research team, ask yourself the following questions:

- Do I like to do research alone or in a group?
- Do I like to discuss my ideas with others or develop them alone or with key informants?
- How well do I work under supervision?
- Am I willing to participate in joint data collection, coding, and analysis?
- Am I willing to share authorship with one or more others?
- Am I a loner?

All ethnographers must work in a social context and be skilled communicators. The list above has less to do with communication and more to do with degree of need for individual ownership of ethnographic data, the field situation, and the products of the research. With willingness to share, many people enjoy the social and intellectual challenge of team ethnography, especially those who have had the benefit of participating in an ethnographic field school as undergraduates or graduate students.

BUILDING INTERDISCIPLINARY
RESEARCH PARTNERSHIPS

What Is an Interdisciplinary Research Partnership?

Today, the paradigms that provide guidance to social science researchers argue strongly for interdisciplinary work. Theoretically driven empirical research, for example, readily uses the input of anthropologists, sociologists, psychologists, epidemiologists, social workers, and physicians. Any researchers concerned about the dilemma of AIDS or the improvement of school performance must take into consideration individual behaviors and motivations as well as structural barriers to effective decision making. To do so rigorously, and with a sufficiently large sample, requires calling upon motivational or behavioral psychologists, survey or epidemiological researchers, and sociologists or anthropologists concerned with the broader social, economic, and political contexts of such problems.

Similarly, ecologically oriented researchers who want to examine the interactions between individuals and their environments also must call upon their colleagues from other disciplines to shed light on individual beliefs and behaviors, characteristics of family and peers, structural characteristics of schools and other institutions, and policies that influence people to think and act.

Sociologists involved in network research need the assistance of epidemiologists and biostatisticians to justify their sampling techniques and engage in the mathematical modeling required for proper analysis of network data; they need ethnographers to identify and understand types of social networks in the field; and they need laboratory researchers to identify biological markers of disease. Thus, interdisciplinary work really cannot be avoided much of the time, especially in applied research.

Cross Reference: See Book 1, Chapter 3, for a more detailed discussion of paradigms guiding social science research

Ethnographers generally hold one of two positions in interdisciplinary teams: director or coordinator of interdisciplinary research projects; or staff ethnographer. Each position calls for different skills and responsibilities, and each poses challenges in ensuring the presence and use of ethnographic data.

Developing and Managing an Interdisciplinary Study: Ethnographers as Project Directors

Ethnographers have distinct advantages as developers and managers of interdisciplinary studies:

- They are trained to hold a holistic perspective.
- They recognize the importance of considering social structures in program development and the establishment and maintenance of program infrastructure.
- They accept qualitative and quantitative methods as equally legitimate, and their training promotes sensitivity to interethnic considerations.
- They are flexible and generally have good social and listening skills so that they can negotiate common ground across disciplines.
- They know how to draw on the strengths of other disciplines to solve problems such as sampling protocols and power calculations, explanations for individual and group behavior, and survey design.
- They are quick to identify, and to call for consideration of, contextual or cultural factors that might hinder or enhance the potential for success of a field study.
- They can become skilled in the design of interesting and innovative studies because of their familiarity with community culture and dynamics and because they are concerned with what things mean to the people involved in the study—how they experience the world.

As research directors, they have the dual responsibility of making sure that the study is carried out effectively and that it includes ethnographic research. The latter requires careful attention, for even when ethnographers are directors or principal investigators and can design their own research together with quantitative researchers and laboratory scientists, they may have difficulty persuading their colleagues that ethnographic research can contribute to the study. Funding or grant review guidelines do not always favor ethnographic research, and researchers from other disciplines may not be familiar with the ways that ethnography can contribute to an interdisciplinary study.

The work associated with research administration usually makes it impossible for ethnographer-administrators to do field research, a fact that many find very frustrating. A central aspect of their work, however, is to make sure that there are other ethnographers on the staff of the project who *can* collect ethnographic data. It then becomes the responsibility of the research administrator to integrate the results of ethnography into the larger study.

Interdisciplinary partnerships work well if all of the members of the research team have identified the study problem as important, are clear about their respective roles in the study, and see the interdependence of the data. The ethnographer-administrator's job is to make sure that this happens. When ethnographer-administrators are members of the team that designs the study, they can select research partners who understand and welcome the role of ethnographic research in the study design. In the following example, the lead investigator, an anthropologist, sought out the assistance of educators, epidemiologists, community physicians, and medical geographers to conduct a study of social organization and children's health in a low-income sector of the city of Lima, Peru.

EXAMPLE 2.6   ▬•▬•▬

ETHNOGRAPHERS AS PRINCIPAL INVESTIGATORS OF AN INTERDISCIPLINARY STUDY

Ethnographer Stephen Schensul led an interdisciplinary team of researchers in a study of pediatric health in communities in the northeast quadrant of Lima, Peru. The study team included anthropologists, educators, pediatricians, and medical geographers. The critical issue connecting members of the research team was a commitment to understanding the social context of pediatric health problems in rapidly changing social environments. Anthropologists on the team situated the study in a series of shanty towns that were evolving into stable communities. Pediatricians familiar with the geographic area and some of the communities, as well as with the epidemiology of the area, provided critical information about childhood diseases and the locations of key informants (such as community health volunteers) knowledgeable about children's diseases. Anthropologists working with a Peruvian educator and pediatricians designed a series of elicitation tools used in ranking children's health problems across communities. Anthropologists and pediatricians working together carried out rapid ethnographic assessments of 20 communities in the target geographic area that included surveys of social organization and infrastructural features (schools, roads, electricity, water availability, etc.). Epidemiologists created sociogeographic maps of health infrastructure in each of the communities. Elicitation and survey data were used by medical geographers to array the data geographically, demonstrating important variations in social organization, infrastructure, perceptions of disease, and epidemiology of disease in the target communities.

> **Cross Reference:**
> See Book 1, Chapter 4, for a discussion of rapid ethnographic research

> **Cross Reference:**
> See Book 4, Chapter 2, by Cromley on the use of maps in ethnographic research

▬•▬•▬

The next case shows how characteristics of a lead researcher—a Spanish, bilingual anthropologist with a nursing degree—led to access to two constituencies critical in conducting her study: interdisciplinary researchers working in the area of diabetes, and Latino patients and their families.

➤•➤•➤   **EXAMPLE 2.7**

AN ANTHROPOLOGIST/NURSE AS PRINCIPAL INVESTIGATOR OF AN INTERDISCIPLINARY STUDY

Henrietta Bernal is an anthropologist, a registered nurse, and a member of the Nursing Faculty of the University of Connecticut. Between 1993 and 1997, she conducted research on the management of diabetes among Puerto Rican older adults in Connecticut, together with nursing faculty and students, anthropologists, an epidemiologist and interviewers at the Institute for Community Research, and nursing staff at the diabetes clinic of a local hospital.

One component of the research involved a baseline survey of insulin-dependent Puerto Rican older women with diabetes to assess the role of social supports and self-efficacy in maintaining regular use of injected insulin. An epidemiologist and biostatistician were important partners in this study. A second component involved partnership with an anthropologist in the development of protocols for proper management of diabetes at home. The anthropologist provided input on dietary advice, contextual factors influencing exercise, and concepts of the body. Nursing staff were trained to conduct the intervention at home and to provide written and oral reports to the principal investigator. Trained ethnographic interviewers visited homes at the beginning and end of the intervention sessions and interviewed women in Spanish to assess treatment satisfaction and barriers to home management.

A third component of Dr. Bernal's work involves a pilot clinical trial of the protocols with a sample of 50 diabetic older Hispanic adults. In this study, 50 adult diabetics will be recruited to the intervention study and will be randomly assigned to a treatment or a control group. The 25 adults in the treatment group will participate in the intervention: seven separate modules for home management of diabetes that will be administered over a 14-week period. The results will be compared to the outcomes in the control group at the end of the program and 4 months later, and the process of implementation will be documented using ethnographic methods. At the end of the 4-month period, the adults in the control group will receive the same intervention, and the results will be assessed at the same points in time (immediately afterward and 4 months later), resulting in a total program sample of 50 adults. The research team is interdisciplinary. In each instance, criteria for selection of the interdisciplinary research team have been their commitment to the issues and their willingness to make use of ethnographic as well as other research methods (Bernal, Woolley, & Schensul, 1997; Bernal, Woolley, Schensul, & Dickinson, 1999).

➤•➤•➤

Managing an interdisciplinary project can present numerous challenges, from negotiating research priorities and methods to the communication and exchanges among participating professionals and institutions. The following illustration shows how such problems emerged in an educational research project investigating technical training needs and skills development in Florida.

EXAMPLE 2.8 ➤•➤•➤

NEGOTIATING INTERDISCIPLINARY AND CROSS-INSTITUTIONAL RESEARCH ON NATIONAL STANDARDS AND THE TRAINING OF SKILLED TECHNICAL WORKERS

Dr. Kathryn Borman, an educational anthropologist at the University of South Florida, co-directs an interdisciplinary team conducting policy research funded by the National Science Foundation (NSF) on national needs for skilled technical graduates. The team consists of faculty and graduate students in applied anthropology and educational research and measurement at the University of South Florida, and administrators and faculty at nearby Indian River Community College. The team has investigated policy issues related to national standards and the training of skilled technical workers. The research also has examined a common core of science, math, engineering, and technology (SMET) skills and competencies needed by industry of 2-year technical graduates. Researchers employ the multiple methods of interviews, observations, specialized sampling methods, and a survey. As co-principal investigator of this project, Dr. Borman guides the development, administration, and evaluation of data collection instruments, including interview and observation protocols, as well as a survey. Additionally, she manages the U.S. team and assists with data collection and analysis.

Several issues and challenges emerged from this collaborative venture. Conflicts erupted early on and often over who should develop and conduct the survey of employers in industries hiring recent graduates from the community college. University collaborators argued that community college faculty should not participate in the survey because they were not trained researchers, and, furthermore, that their objectivity would be compromised because their salaries were supported by these same employers. Community college faculty, believing themselves to be experts in their fields, wanted to review their own curricula rather than bring in outside reviewers or students, as suggested by university-based researchers. The parties struggled over priorities, with university researchers arguing that the NSF was invested only in supporting the education of the graduate students who carried out work in the project, and community college faculty and administration believing that faculty development of community college participants was the most important dimension of training. Both sets of participants were probably correct because the project was funded jointly by two divisions in the NSF—one having responsibility for research in education and the other invested in assisting community colleges in making extensive changes in their curriculum and instructional approaches. Throughout these struggles, the research team remained together and is currently writing a book titled *Training Postmodern Workers: Skills and High-Tech Work in the Sunbelt.*

➤•➤•➤

When the Ethnographer Is a Member of the Interdisciplinary Research Team

Depending on the reason for including ethnographers on a research team, inclusion of ethnographic data in a study may be more difficult when ethnographers are members of a research team but not the directors or principal investigators. It is important to know why the team hired ethnographers before deciding to join it. Such reasons may include the following:

- The principal investigators were told to hire ethnographers by the funding agency.

- The principal investigators know little or nothing about the community or population they wish to study, and they do not know how to learn about it.

- The principal investigators view the community or setting in which the people they wish to study live as dangerous and would like to have as members of the team researchers who have already established relationships with the community.

- The researchers would like to be able to explain their quantitative study results better.

- The research team would like to adapt instruments and other data collection techniques to the communities in which they propose to work.

- The target population/communities are ethnically or culturally diverse, and ethnographers are needed to assist in identifying important aspects of cultural diversity for the study.

- Self-report by research participants does not provide adequate information about behaviors that constitute the subject of the study, and observation and in-depth interviews are required.

- Approaches to intervention are not effective, and researchers want to know why.

Cross Reference:
See Book 1 for a discussion of the kinds of questions for which ethnography is an appropriate design choice

Definition: Cultural brokering refers to translating information from one socio/cultural group to another including conveying opinions and negotiating priorities

The first four reasons call for **cultural brokering** between researchers and study communities. We do not advise ethnographers to act as cultural brokers between the study community and other researchers unless they are certain that the research team will be receptive to study results (cf. Chambers, 1987; Schensul & Schensul, 1978). As cultural brokers, ethnographers have limited power and control over the uses of their research. Their presence on the team is required primarily because the rest of the research team has little capacity to interact directly with the target population and would prefer to assign that responsibility to the community experts. However, researchers who lack experience with the target population will not necessarily gain it by reading ethnographers' reports. Thus, ethnographers' efforts at disseminating their research within the study or advocating effectively may well fail. At the same time, the communities in which the ethnographers are establishing relationships will surely make demands on the researchers, the project, and the employee institution. These demands may not be met because either the team leaders did not anticipate them and did not build associated costs into the project budget, or they did not wish to heed the ethnographers' advice. Thus, ethnographers are liable to find themselves advocating on behalf of the communities in which they are conducting their research rather than brokering research information between the communities and institutions.

The last four reasons—improving instruments, enhancing cultural responsiveness, sharing research results with the community, and improving intervention results—are all indicators that the interdisciplinary research team is prepared to use the results of ethnography to improve the research and will promote a positive relationship between the research team and the community in question. In these settings, a team of ethnographers is more likely to achieve success.

➤•➤•➤ **EXAMPLE 2.9**

CONDUCTING ETHNOGRAPHY WITH INJECTION DRUG USERS IN MIAMI AS A MEMBER OF AN INTERDISCIPLINARY RESEARCH TEAM

As the Atlanta-based Centers for Disease Control began to recognize that HIV was infecting injection drug users, the U.S. National Institute on Drug Abuse (NIDA) made research resources available to university-based and other researchers to conduct street outreach and intervention with men and women who were using drugs intravenously, as well as their sex partners. Dr. Bryan Page, an ethnographer with the School of Psychiatry at the University of Miami, joined the research team headed by Dr. Clyde McCoy, a physician. Page's assignment was to get to know and to interview injection drug users in the field. Like other anthropologists involved in similar studies, he was to contribute his descriptive findings to epidemiological researchers and interventionists, who would then use the results to target better research questions, more effective outreach strategies, and more culturally focused intervention.

Dr. Page's challenge was to find ways of communicating his ethnographic findings about relationships among injection drug users, patterns of drug use that were more likely to transmit HIV, and barriers to communication about risk prevention (e.g., using a condom or suggesting safer sexual behaviors) to epidemiologists and interventionists who could not readily change their previously defined measurement tools and intervention strategies.

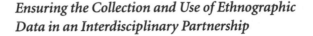

Ensuring the Collection and Use of Ethnographic Data in an Interdisciplinary Partnership

Administrators and team researchers who are ethnographers face different challenges in ensuring the collection and use of data in interdisciplinary studies. They must do the following:

- Maintain their credibility as ethnographers with the ethnographers they hire and supervise
- Maintain their credibility as ethnographers to their colleagues in other settings who are involved directly in ethnographic research
- Find comfortable ways to incorporate ethnographic data that they did not personally collect into their own publications

Ethnographer-administrators can conceptualize and seek funding for projects that incorporate ethnography as a central component of the study, thereby ensuring its value to the research team. At the same time, they are in a strong position to be able to guide ethnographic research so that it has obvious connections with other data collection methods. They also can explain and promote ethnography as an approach to research to team members from other disciplines. Finally, they can link or triangulate ethnographic with other types of data collected by the project, creating a conceptually integrated picture.

Unless team leaders truly understand the role that ethnographic research can play in a study, ethnographers working as team members often find themselves marching to a different drummer. They will tend to veer toward investigating cultural patterning, collecting narratives of experience, and defining their own interests. Whereas ethnographers do what they often do—work to answer new questions not originally asked in the project—researchers from other disciplines may have different expectations regarding their role. Often, they expect ethnographers to educate them about community of study, thereby shielding anyone but the designated ethnographer from interacting with members of the community. Nonethnographers may consider the ethnographer's work to be of secondary importance and therefore may devote less time, money, and interest to ethnographic investigation. Under these circumstances, many ethnographers begin to avoid the members of their own team, using the opportunity to conduct their own research. Such circumstances do not result in productive research collaborations.

To ensure collection and use of ethnographic data in an interdisciplinary study, ethnographers on the staff should be able to do the following:

- Instruct the lead investigators on the formats and uses of ethnographic research
- Work with investigators to identify where ethnographic research can play a role in the study, and how it can link with the study context, study hypotheses, instrument development, and explanation of research results
- Collect ethnographic data using interviews, observational methods, elicitation techniques, and other means relevant to domains in the conceptual framework guiding the study and/or domains reflected in quantitative instruments to be used in the study
- Identify ethnographic substudies that will investigate new issues arising from the ongoing research about which little or nothing is known

Interdisciplinary Intervention Studies

Some interdisciplinary partnerships involve intervention studies. Intervention studies are usually organized to test a theoretically driven program that is intended to change the behavior of individuals or groups in a predictable manner. Hundreds of such studies have been designed to test new instructional methods in schools; new ways of preventing adolescent risk behavior; and more effective approaches to improving access to health care for infants and young children, among other things. Intervention studies are usually, although not always, interdisciplinary; for this reason, many of the same considerations mentioned with respect to ethnographers' roles in interdisciplinary research projects apply to intervention studies.

Cross Reference: Book 7, Chapter 1

There are, however, exceptions in intervention studies that cause particular dilemmas for ethnographers. These stem from two sources: (a) Ethnographers are usually hired to conduct the formative research, which will contribute to the formation of the intervention. Often, intervention studies are guided by preselected theoretical approaches drawn from other fields that do not readily adjust to new informational inputs. The information brought to the intervention program by the ethnographer may be viewed as irrelevant to the planned approach or not readily integrated into its theoretical components. (b) Ethnographers involved in process evaluations may find that what they observe is inconsistent with the intention of the intervention. Thus, they are potentially in the position of bringing bad news to the project or to the funder. Finally, ethnographers may be able to choose whether they would like to contribute to project formation, process or outcome evaluation, or all three. To foresee these problems and to choose the best intervention study fit, ethnographers should consider the following questions:

- Does the ethnographer prefer that the research be immediately valuable to the research site (formative research and process evaluation), or for purposes of disseminating results to a larger audience (outcome evaluation)?

- At what stage of development is the intervention study? Is it too late to include results of formative research?

- Does the ethnographer like to work on a team that includes intervention as well as research staff?

- What stresses, if any, exist between implementation and evaluation staff on the project, and to what extent might this affect the work of ethnographers on the team?

- Is the overall study design one that meets with the ethnographer's expectations regarding scientific rigor *and* responsiveness to the target population?

- Will the ethnographer feel comfortable conducting the intended research with the target population and designated research team?

Of these questions, the most important is the last.

Ethical and Human Subject Issues in Ethnographic or Interdisciplinary Research Teams

The circumstances of ethnographic field research are different from other research designs that depend more on objective or outsider observations of behavior, or self-reports from participants through surveys. How ethnographers exercise judgment in the field to ensure ethical procedures in the research process is as important as the rules of informed consent well known in survey or epidemiological research. Ethnographers may be involved in observing social settings that include large numbers of people who cannot be asked for informed consent. They interview key informants repeatedly rather than once, as in survey research. They may observe or hear about behaviors that are illegal, or reportable by law. They may be asked to participate in illegal

Cross Reference: Chapter 1, this volume, on the researcher's role

activities, such as purchasing or holding drugs for informants. Field situations evolve; the circumstances of the research are not always predictable in advance. Ethnographers often have personal relationships with respondents/key informants, and the legal issues displayed in an informed consent form may be insulting or frightening to respondents or culturally inappropriate. Thus, the conditions under which informed consent is sought, confidentiality is maintained, and the health and well-being of the research participants are protected are somewhat different—but no less rigorous—for ethnographers than for quantitative researchers whose work depends on standardized single interviews or surveys conducted in office settings. These differences and ethical and human subject issues are discussed more fully in Chapter 1 of this book and in Book 1, Chapter 8. Here, we mention several issues that take on special importance when ethnographers are working in team settings, managing confidentiality, and ensuring informed consent.

Cross Reference: Book 1, Chapter 8, and Chapter 1, this volume

Managing confidentiality in fieldnotes in team research. Sharing ethnographic fieldnotes with a team of researchers creates several problems related to confidentiality and the protection of study participants. The first is the identity of the informant. Team field research often requires that team members know the true identity of all participants to avoid duplicate interviewing, compare reports made to different team members in different contexts, or complement each other's field observations and interviews to create the fullest picture possible. However, this may present ethical conflicts. For example, a key informant may disclose personal information or information about an illegal or violent incident (e.g., child abuse or a murder) to a member of the team by virtue of the rapport established between them. Should the team member share this information? In what form can it be shared that protects the identity of the person who conveyed it? How should it be portrayed in the field-notes? What should the team member do with this information?

Some suggestions for mediating dilemmas such as these are the following:

- Fieldnotes should be protected when necessary by a federal certificate of confidentiality, which ensures that fieldnotes cannot be subpoenaed for use in court or by a grand jury.
- Key informants should never be named as sources of information in fieldnotes or in public settings.
- Information received from one respondent should always be cross-checked or validated through reports from others.
- Team members from other disciplines should be trained to understand ethnographic research, principles of informed consent, and protection of human subjects in the context of ethnography.

Cross Reference: Chapter 1, this volume, describes these issues in detail

Informed Consent. The second important ethical issue to be considered in a team context is informed consent. Ethnographers must explain the concept of informed consent and protection of human subjects to research participants in language they can understand. At the same time, the standards and guidelines for obtaining informed consent in survey and clinical research may not apply to ethnographic research or to the communities in which the research is to be conducted. Ethnographers should raise and discuss these discrepancies and negotiate compromises that honor the requirements of institutional review boards and the cultural constraints and demands of the research communities.

Cross Reference: Chapter 1, this volume

Definition: Informed consent is the participant's formal consent to participate in the research after being fully informed about the study design, process and uses of the data, risks and benefits of participation, and mechanisms for protecting confidentiality

To ensure **informed consent**, participants in an ethnographic or interdisciplinary study need to be told that information that they provide will be available to a larger research team, which will consider the information confidential. The participants need to be reassured that whatever they say and do, although shared with other research team members, will not result in any harm to them, their families, or their communities.

Perhaps the most important thing to remember is that personal relationships lie at the heart of the ethnographic endeavor. In the context of these relationships, ethnographers are obliged to maximize benefit and minimize risk to the communities in which they work. This requires more than just informing communities of the research purposes and procedures. Because ethnographers generally understand reciprocity (and know that communities sometimes expect and demand it), they generally go beyond responsible informing to offer whatever service they can to members of the research community (Omidian & Lipson, 1996).

EXAMPLE 2.10 ◆•◆•◆

PROVIDING RECIPROCAL SERVICES TO AN ARTS EDUCATION COMMUNITY

Margaret LeCompte, an ethnographer and evaluator; Debra Holloway, a literacy specialist; and Wendy Maybin, a statistician and mathematician, worked as a team with a group of public school teachers who wanted to learn how to infuse the arts throughout their varied subject areas, which range from history and social studies to math and physical education. The teachers wanted to organize a seminar to explore these issues, but they did not have anyone to guide them. Holloway volunteered to lead the group, and both she and LeCompte located readings and identified speakers and consultants for their weekly classes. All three researchers monitored the teachers' activities, maintaining a historical record of their progress—something the teachers wanted to do but for which they lacked the time. LeCompte designed the monitoring procedures, and Maybin designed a system for tracking the impact of teacher innovations on students.

Defining the boundaries between appropriate and inappropriate reciprocity lies at the heart of the dialogue regarding ethical considerations in ethnographic research (Marshall, in press; Singer et al., in press). In team research, coming to agreement on these definitions is critical in order to avoid different responses to respondents' needs, which create discord among ethnographers and competition among respondents for ethnographers' time and other resources.

Now that we have considered ethnographic and interdisciplinary partnerships, we turn our attention to the challenges of building a third type of partnership that involves both researchers and nonresearchers who are concerned about solving a pressing problem, resolving inequities in the distribution of social resources, or improving conditions for the benefit of their constituencies. We refer to these as action research partnerships.

BUILDING ACTION RESEARCH PARTNERSHIPS

What Is an Action Research Partnership?

Building action research partnerships is an explicit strategy to ensure that (a) research applied to community development or change involves and responds to the diversity of participants in the community setting; and (b) community or institutional change efforts are informed and therefore proactive rather than reactive. **Action research** involves researchers and nonresearch partners in joint problem definition, selection of research methods, data collection, analysis, and plans and actions for use.

Action research is, by definition, a partnership. An action research partnership should include from the outset researchers and action-oriented partners from the community (or institutions) involved in the study. The partnership is important because:

Definition: Action research is problem-oriented research carried out by action-oriented researchers and community or institutional partners that is designed to bring about a desired change, the direction of which is guided by the research results

■ It ensures that the research questions asked are relevant to the concerns of each of the constituencies.

■ It requires consensus among partners regarding research questions and the issues they are to address in order to move forward.

■ It ensures the involvement of community representatives in information collection, analysis and use, and goal definition.

There are other advantages to an action research partnership. For example, researchers cannot be familiar with all of the communities, sectors, or cultural settings and meanings that must be considered in the project. Working with community leaders or organizations can provide entry to diverse communities and more comprehensive and relevant understanding of the community setting in which the research and related change or development strategies are to take place. *Participatory action research produces better knowledge for better "action"—improved services, better education, or changes in policies.*

 Key point

 Key point

Intersectoral approaches are critical to community problem solving. Current thinking on the efficacy of interventions suggests that interventions are most effective when they influence several different levels or sectors (e.g., school, community, and family) at the same time (cf. Bronfenbrenner, 1977; Dryfoos, 1990; Hawkins, Catalano, & Miller, 1992; Nastasi & DeZolt, 1994). The projects that form the basis for discussing ethnographic contributions to program interventions in Book 7 involve working with individuals (young adults, or young girls and their mothers); groups (of youth, girls, caregivers); community organizations; university-trained researchers; and other agencies at the same time. Each of the sectors most involved in the issues should be represented in an action research partnership. The following example illustrates the role of action research in building a community partnership and the importance of good facilitation in maintaining it.

Cross Reference: Book 7, Chapter 1, on the contributions of ethnographic research to program interventions

BUILDING A PEACE PARK WITH A MULTISECTOR ACTION RESEARCH PARTNERSHIP

Beth Krensky is an artist, educator, and activist, as well as the co-founder of Project Yes, a nonprofit organization that brings at-risk youth into arts activities that help them develop a stronger sense of identity and the survival skills to stay in school. Searching for a way to use the arts to reduce neighborhood violence, Krensky has developed a project in which youths living in a community long troubled with intergroup and interethnic conflict will construct a Peace Park. Krensky has worked to build the coalition that has established and supported the Peace Park; her doctoral dissertation research will document its development and the impact that creating and using the park has on youthful participants and the community at large. Her research will also help to build a model for other communities wishing to engage in such projects.

Initial partners were Project Yes, with its expertise in mobilizing groups of youth to work together; KaBoom!, a national nonprofit organization that provides technical assistance in fund-raising, planning, and public relations for community projects—such as playgrounds—that enhance the lives of residents in low-income neighborhoods; Learning Structures, a firm of innovative playground architects that Project Yes had selected to design the Peace Park using ideas elicited from groups of local youth; and the University of Colorado, whose graduate and undergraduate students serve as mentors to young people with whom Project Yes works.

Finding a site, however, proved difficult. Many communities feared having youths with a history of conflict working together. Owners of many apartment complexes refused to sponsor such an activity. Finally, the Lafitte Gardens community, which needed a playground/park, asked Project Yes to help them create one. Krensky then had to recruit as a partner the local middle school, because she wanted the young people who were to participate in creating the park to receive service-learning credit for designing the park and leading groups of volunteer workers during the building phase. Several teachers from the school had to be convinced to use the Peace Park Project as their fall service-learning project. Additional partners were recruited among local businesses and municipal departments for volunteers, funds, and other forms of material support. None of these entities or individuals—architects, consultants, Project Yes, apartment complex and community leaders, educators, students, businesses, and community agencies—had worked together before, and few had any experience with using the arts as a means for inducing social change. Krensky, as overall project director, had to serve as a go-between and culture broker, helping each to achieve needed goals while working more or less in concert.

➤━●━➤━●━➤

Key point   Research is improved by the importance and urgency of the topic it addresses. *The quality of a research effort is improved when community partnerships are intensely committed to the results and therefore to ensuring the quality of the research.* Furthermore, intense commitment means that differences of opinion in substance and method that may arise among researchers and their partners are likely to be thoroughly analyzed, discussed, debated, and resolved in the context of important community problem solving. Recognizing and addressing these differences provides important information to researchers and, at the same time, can help partners deal with internal and cross-community or cross-agency conflicts. When research combines with good facilitation and the ability to relate to deep-seated emotional responses to difference, it can offer a powerful set of tools for improving communication required to carry out action partnerships.

Building and Maintaining Action Research Partnerships

Key point   For researchers to be effective in influencing the creation of an action research partnership, they must be sufficiently involved in the life of the target community to have some idea of which topics are of interest, and which individuals might be called together to discuss these topics. *Thus, the first step for a committed action researcher in a partnership effort is involvement in the local community or communities in which research may take place.*

━•━•━ **EXAMPLE 2.12**

IDENTIFYING TOPICS THAT INTEREST ALL MEMBERS OF A COMMUNITY

In Example 2.10, we described how a multidisciplinary research team provided services that members of the educational community felt they needed. LeCompte and her team had, however, been working with the Arts Focus program, of which the teachers were a part, for 2 years before they felt comfortable enough to know when to volunteer specific services. During those 2 years, the researchers had helped teachers chaperone field trips, build sets for theatre programs, record and reproduce minutes at meetings, and write grant proposals to help the program obtain funds. They also had been sympathetic listeners to overworked teachers during a time of administrative and political upheaval in the school district. As a consequence, they did not hesitate when teachers finally asked them to take a more leading role in staff development that the teachers' seminar entailed—even though their original role had been more supportive and reactive than proactive.

━•━•━

Ethnographers who wish to conduct action research programs generally begin by entering one or more such local communities and identifying a number of distinctive programs and/or key leaders or contacts. Entry should follow the usual procedures outlined in a good ethnography text, including identification of key informants or knowledgeable people; attendance at (and participation in) important meetings; interviews with school personnel or agency heads; reviews of local newspapers; and talks with community residents, parents, teachers, service providers, artists, and so on.

Cross Reference:
See Book 2, Chapter 4, and Chapter 1, this volume, for more information on entering research settings

For action researchers, however, these entry methods take on an additional level of importance because researchers are seeking to identify important actors in relation to selected topics, as well as to uncover important orienting information.

Key point

Key point   *It is very important to assess through ethnographic research which organizations, individuals, and networks are likely to be interested in participating in a research or evaluation project.* They constitute the building blocks of an action research partnership, providing the foundation for a variety of different initiatives.

Once the community has been approached, important components of the partnership must be put into place. Some of the most important components of a successful action research partnership are the following:

- An experienced facilitator or researcher/actor team as convener
- Careful definition of partners
- Ability to integrate research with service, policy, or other agendas of partners
- Clarity of cultural content, and culturally representative membership
- Equitable exchange of resources
- Ability to broker funding
- Ability to negotiate the roles of collaborating members

Experienced facilitator. The first important criterion for success is the selection of an experienced or knowledgeable facilitator. The facilitator of the action research team should know enough about the participating sectors of the community to be sensitive to **key stakeholders** and to make sure that they are involved in the earliest planning stages.

Definition: Stakeholders are those who are affected by the problem and the proposed work of the action research team

Facilitation skills and knowledge of the community are necessary but not sufficient to guarantee the facilitator success in group management and positive outcomes. Social class, racial or ethnic identity, perceived power, gender, perceived access to resources, and institutional affiliation in relation to group membership of partners will make a difference in the ability of the facilitator to manage the group. The facilitator's power may be contested, and the facilitator may have to be replaced.

Furthermore, facilitators usually have vested interests—they will invest time and effort in the development of a group project if they or their institution sees the potential of material or other gain. It is always helpful if a facilitator identifies his or her vested interests early in the process so that he or she cannot be accused of having a hidden personal agenda.

Defining and Selecting Partners

Who should be included? The group should consider carefully who should be included in the initial planning stages or along the way. Inviting the wrong partners (those who are likely to offer obstacles to a project from the beginning or who may undermine efforts to obtain funding) is a disadvantage in the early stages of a partnership, although sometimes it is better to involve potential critics from the beginning rather than after a project has been developed. Decisions in favor of inclusion should rest on the potential scope of the project, the resources available, political implications of exclusion, and number of agencies and individuals with whom the facilitator can work comfortably. Sometimes, a partnership includes only two or three organizations. At other times, it may include many more. Partnerships should connect service/advocacy and research.

Integration of Research With Service, Advocacy, and Policy. The ability to make the connections among service delivery, advocacy and policy change, and research activities is critical to the stability of a partnership and to ensuring the central role of research in it. The facilitator should be familiar with the priorities of service providers, administrators, educators, health personnel, or community leaders, and should be able to speak to and support these priorities while promoting the integration of research into program planning. Because research is sometimes viewed as an unnecessary or undesirable appendage to program services (Schensul, in press; Schensul & Schensul, 1992; Schensul, Donelli-Hess, & Martinez, 1987), it is critical to demonstrate to doubting service personnel early on that information collection can be immediately useful to their work and should be integrated into it.

Clarity of cultural orientation and representation. Initiators should decide early on what the cultural content of the project should be—for example, whether the project will be multiethnic and multicultural in its approach, and in what ways the development and implementation of multicultural interventions should be addressed.

Action research efforts may choose to develop or explore levels of cultural relevance. Because historical accuracy has not yet been achieved, and many dimensions of national and ethnic histories remain uncovered, even ethnic minority organizations may not be well informed about the cultural and historical features of their constituencies. Community educators and interventionists must learn to identify these characteristics and to reconstruct history in order to build culturally appropriate interventions. It is critical to remember that "culture" is not monolithic. Each target population may have its own cultural profile within a specific ethnic/cultural or social group. Mexican Americans in Chicago, for example, self-differentiate by generation and place of origin (Southwest, Midwest, or location in Mexico). Puerto Ricans in the northeastern United States differ in many ways from their counterparts in Puerto Rico, and among Puerto Ricans, there are important cultural differences depending on time and place of birth, migration pat-

Cross Reference: See Book 1, Chapter 1, for a discussion of the importance of recognizing intracultural differences in research communities; also see Book 7, Chapter 3, for a discussion of approaches to these issues and several multiethnic, multicultural projects

terns, and language use. Ongoing assessment of cultural characteristics and culture change should be built into the job
descriptions of all project staff. Another way to state this prin-
ciple is to say that every population is special and worthy of
research attention by an action research partnership.

Sharing resources. Financial and other incentives and equitable exchange of resources are critical to the success of any
partnership. Involvement in exchanges strengthens institutional commitment to the project. ***Organizations and com-*** **Key point**
munity leaders will participate in action research efforts
when incentives are strong and attractive. Partnership
building can make use of incentives, which may be financial,
social, or political. Agreements on sharing resources and the
meaning of incentives must be confirmed in writing to
avoid misunderstandings later. Commitment to the effort
is greatly strengthened when all participating organizations
identify concretely both what they hope to gain and what
contributions they can make to the program.

Resources that consortium partners can bring to bear on
a project can include the following:

- Money or in-kind services (copying or printing, mailing and
  postage)
- Time to foster communications among consortium members
- A network of volunteers
- Relationships with the press, and public relations skills
- Meeting space and expenses
- Ability to conduct focus group interviews
- Data
- Computer skills

EXAMPLE 2.13 ━●━●━●

CONTRIBUTING ORGANIZATIONAL RESOURCES TO AN ACTION RESEARCH PARTNERSHIP

In 1997, the Institute for Community Research (ICR) sought and received funding from the National Institute of Mental Health for support for its Summer Youth Research Institute (SYRI). The SYRI provides an intensive 6-week paid internship for urban high school students who focus on action research problems in health (AIDS, reproductive health, and violence) and education. Partners with the ICR in the application and the program are the University of Connecticut's (UCONN) Center for International Community Health Studies (CICHS) and Office of Minority Student Programs, Yale University's Center for Interdisciplinary Research on AIDS (CIRA), Central Connecticut State University's Department of Anthropology, and the City of Hartford's Summer Youth Employment Program. An additional partner in 1998 was the Connecticut Children's Medical Center Pediatric AIDS Program. Each of the partners offered the program specific resources. CICHS provided a computer laboratory and training in data management; and the UCONN Office of Minority Student Programs provided opportunities for SYRI participants and UCONN Summer Scientists students to meet, as well as student scholarships. The Pediatric AIDS program contributed students and paid scholarships. Hartford SYRI participants were supported full-time for 6 weeks through the Hartford Summer Youth Employment Program, and Yale School of Public Health and Central Connecticut State University faculty provided opportunities for students to visit their campuses and learn about educational opportunities for the future.

━●━●━●

Brokering funding possibilities. Research networks need financial support (cf. Omidian & Lipson, 1996, p. 359). Researchers who wish to form consortia must offer ideas sufficiently compelling to bind the network into a joint vision and mission and to serve as a platform for seeking funding. Ideally, funding sources should be identified in advance. The partnership can then work together on a proposal for research and intervention. It is quite difficult to develop an action research partnership if no thought is given in advance to sources of financial support. *Leaders of* **Key point** *the partnership can expect no more than two chances to obtain necessary financial support before the partners may become discouraged and drift away.* Once disappointment sets in, it is difficult to rekindle enthusiasm for continuing the work.

Generally, however, it is easier to move ahead with consortium planning when financial resources are available to support meetings, minutes, mailings, and the search for longer-term funding. Decisions about the allocation of resources during the planning period, and after projects are funded, should be made jointly and with the agreement of all partners. Misunderstandings about money are highly detrimental to the viability of action research partnerships because of the high level of distrust that exists between communities and/or nonresearchers and the research establishment.

Sometimes, projects must adapt to the interests of funders, requiring changes in the goals and objectives of the action research partnership, as illustrated in the following examples.

━●━●━● **EXAMPLE 2.14**

AIDS INTERVENTION OR AIDS KNOWLEDGE
ATTITUDES AND BEHAVIOR SURVEY?

In 1988, three community organizations (the Institute for Community Research, the Hispanic Health Council, and the Urban League of Greater Hartford) and the local health department formed a consortium to address the problem of HIV/AIDS in the city of Hartford.

The intention of the group was to approach the Centers for Disease Control (CDC) for discretionary funding for a demonstration intervention with an evaluation. At the point at which the group was ready to request funding, the CDC decided to decentralize national HIV resources to each of the states in the form of block grants. At the same time, the CDC was committed to locally administered Knowledge, Attitude and Behavior (KAB) surveys using a standardized instrument developed in conjunction with the World Health Organization to provide baseline data in states. The Connecticut State Department of Health shifted the agenda of the group from research and intervention with a group known to be at risk of infection through injection drug use to a Knowledge, Attitudes and Behavior study of a random sample of residents between the ages of 18 and 49 believed to be sexually active in identified high- and lower-risk neighborhoods of the city. The consortium agreed to accept funding for the Knowledge, Attitudes and Behavior study with the hope that it would provide the basis for generating a much-needed citywide intervention. Ultimately, two such studies were completed, and findings were used successfully in seeking both research and direct intervention funding from a variety of sources (AIDS Community Research Group, 1988, 1989).

⬤➤⬤➤

The following illustrates how local funding sources can lead a group of organizations with one purpose to support another.

EXAMPLE 2.15   ⬤➤⬤➤

PREVENTION OR INTERVENTION?

Early work of the Hispanic Health Council had demonstrated that otitis media (middle ear infection) was a critical problem in Hartford, especially for Puerto Rican children between birth and 5 years of age. Otitis media, if not effectively treated, can cause intermittent, and sometimes permanent, hearing loss, which, if not detected, can result in delays in language and cognitive development (Allen, 1988; Schensul, 1983, 1996).

The Hispanic Health Council believed that one way of addressing this problem was to test for hearing loss by outfitting a mobile van with audiological assessment equipment and a soundproof room, and it was negotiating with a local community foundation for the purchase of such a van and the staff to conduct testing and education around prevention of hearing loss.

Meanwhile, through the special learning needs subcommittee of an early childhood education consortium, the Institute for Community Research was preparing a consortium-based proposal for a mobile van to conduct parent education around cognitive, language, and developmental delays in young children.

After studying both proposals, the local foundation brought the two groups together with the mission of creating a joint proposal for an audiological screening van with soundproof room and sophisticated audiological equipment. The project included a significantly reduced community education component. The staff of the project encountered many problems in obtaining the equipment and making sure it functioned effectively, and in recruiting and assessing enough children to make it cost-effective. Ultimately, in accordance with the wishes of the foundation and the successful completion of the pilot effort, the project was transferred to Medicaid funding.

Approximately 10% of the children screened had hearing impairments at the time of the screening, and approximately 5% had hearing impairments of sufficient magnitude that they required some form of medication or intervention. The mobile van performed a valuable service for children already affected, but staff were unable to find the time to engage in preventive education on early identification of cognitive impairments and learning delays with parents. Nearly a decade later, the mobile van is still in operation, but parents in the community still do not have sufficient information about early childhood development or where to go for services if they need them (Schensul, 1996).

━●━●━●

Negotiating the roles of collaborating members. The roles, responsibilities, and expectations of each of the organizations in an action research partnership should be clarified early (even before a project officially begins) and preferably in writing, if a collaboration is to run smoothly. Regular review of the status of each of the organizations is beneficial in avoiding misunderstandings and unmet expectations.

Limited resources usually preclude duplication of services. Thus, conflicts may arise among organizations in the consortium that play similar roles in the community with respect to who should participate and toward what end. Whenever possible, potential sources of conflict should be identified and addressed early. Avoiding disagreements with respect to membership can be managed if consortium guidelines are created that specify the number of organizations of each type required in a consortium. Another option is to specify the skills and services needed in the partnership. By specifying the parameters of the project early in the process, organizations can self-select to participate or to drop out.

EXAMPLE 2.16 ━━•━━•━━

DECIDING TO LEAVE A RESEARCH PARTNERSHIP

In the early stages of its development, the Hartford VIP (Violence Intervention Project) needed a 24-hour hotline, access to emergency rooms, good relationships with the police department, and a consortium of service organizations to provide backup services to children affected by violence. Evaluation was considered to be of secondary importance, and research on violence was not at all interesting to consortium members at this point. These needs and sentiments among consortium members resulted in a decision on the part of a member research organization to decrease its involvement in the project and, eventually, to drop out.

━━•━━•━━

Participating organizations generally have agendas, policies, and needs. These should be spelled out contractually or in letters of agreement in advance, or they may come into conflict with the overall program and intentions of the partnership, thus threatening its integrity. Regardless of careful forethought, differences of opinion or interest may arise during the life of a partnership, as the following examples illustrate.

⬛•⬛•⬛ **EXAMPLE 2.17**

WHEN THE GOALS OF ONE OR MORE OF THE PARTNERS COME INTO CONFLICT WITH THE GOALS OF THE PROJECT

LeCompte had spent several years working with school district personnel to help them develop a curriculum and set of instructional strategies compatible with the culture of the American Indian students who constituted 97% of the students in the district. The project's rather ambitious goals involved using existing ethnographic data, as well as data newly generated in the community, to design culturally appropriate materials for all of the subject areas, as well as to identify indigenous strategies for teaching and learning that could be adapted for use in public school classrooms. The project was informed by research that indicated that Indian students who knew about and felt proud of their own culture were more likely to complete high school, and that schools that ignored or denigrated Indian culture created high drop-out rates among Indian students.

LeCompte had secured a grant to support some of the work, but progress was slow. The superintendent of the school district had hoped that the project would "put the district on the map" and help him achieve more visibility as an educational leader. After 3 years, the superintendent grew impatient and joined forces with a conservative policy group whose educational agenda emphasized teaching all students content dominated by Western European history, literature, language, and social studies. Arguing that studying the same things that European American students did would bring Indian students into the mainstream quickly—and that the policy group had a ready-made curriculum the district could adopt immediately—the superintendent ended efforts to implement a culturally compatible curriculum by changing district priorities

⬛•⬛•⬛

Each time a new organization or group is brought into a partnership, the history, rationale, guidelines for participation, and role of each member of the network should be reiterated. Attention given to transitions in and out of partnerships will pay off handsomely in the end by reducing distrust and retaining potential for new partnership relations in the future.

The situations of participating organizations may shift and change at any time during the implementation of a program. These changes may affect the mission, direction, resource level, supervisory capacity, reputation, and other dimensions of the institution. Any such changes, such as the loss of an agency director or key staff, funding shortages, or a shift in agency policies and priorities should be identified, discussed, studied, and renegotiated as they occur. Partnership leaders should communicate these changes and their implications to the rest of the consortium in order to avoid gossip and misunderstanding.

EXAMPLE 2.18 ━●━●━●━

WHEN ORGANIZATIONAL GOALS CHANGE IN MIDSTREAM TO
CONFLICT WITH THE GOALS OF THE RESEARCH PARTNERSHIP

Urban Women Against Substance Abuse, an intervention study designed to reduce drug-, sex-, and violence-related risk behavior in preadolescent girls, was developed by the Institute for Community Research in conjunction with three community advocacy/service organizations. The intention of the community partnership component of the study was to reinforce individual and group norms' change by involving girls and their caregivers in community action projects targeted to raising awareness of drug use as a problem to be prevented in their own communities. The program, along with the community action component, was then designed to be institutionalized in the participating community agencies. Several conditions were required for community institutionalization—space, time and staff resources to participate in the program, and organizational interest in substance abuse prevention in the community.

During the first program year, project staff began to work with one of the three community organizations. This organization was highly sympathetic to the program, and the director had been part of the team that had developed the program design. Furthermore, the director had also been an active participant in an antecedent action research training program for community women—the Urban Women's Development Project—and had learned in this program how to conduct research and use the results to advocate and promote changes in policies affecting women.

The organization offered space, transportation, and recruitment assistance to the UWASA program, and the director attended and helped to facilitate focus group sessions with residents of the community and their preadolescent daughters, in preparation for the program year.

Shortly after the program year began, the relationship between the director of the organization and the board of directors became conflictual. The roots of the conflict lay in a difference of opinion between the director and the board over whether the organization should become involved in developing low- and moderate-income housing. The director's primary concern was stabilization of the neighborhood through promotion of housing and community development, whereas the board was interested in the provision of social services. The conflict affected the program indirectly because it drew increasingly on the community agency director's time, reducing her availability to the program. In addition, the board's all-or-nothing perspective forced the director into an oppositional stance in favor of active advocacy for housing and community development to the exclusion of service. Seeking support for our combined service, antidrug, and community development program meant working with both the board and the director, who did not see eye to eye on most issues. Eventually, the board of directors forced the director to leave her position. Despite the UWASA program's emphasis on service, it was associated with the former director and did not receive support from the board of directors. Consequently, the program was compelled to seek another, more supportive community base.

━●━●━●

In funded action research partnerships, one partner must act as the **fiduciary agent**, receiving money from the funder(s) and subcontracting with other partners. Collaboration implies equality of partnership, but subcontractual relationships are, by definition, hierarchical, because the fiduciary agent is viewed as—and is technically—responsi-

Definition: A fiduciary agent is an organization that receives and manages money on behalf of other organizations ble for the project. Partners may take great pains to construct equitable partnerships with joint policy and administrative teams, joint planning and decision making, and joint negotiation of budgets. But in the end, if a subcontractor does not comply, the contract must be terminated with the possibility that hostility will be directed toward the fiduciary agency.

EXAMPLE 2.19   ▰▰▰▰▰

DIFFICULTIES RESULTING FROM PARTNERS' INABILITY TO FULFILL COMMITMENTS

One of LeCompte's projects involved helping a very rural school district to build a more stable cadre of teachers. Most of the regular teachers were outsiders who lived for short periods of time in the isolated area but did not plan to stay. Teacher turnover was very high, and both staff morale and student achievement suffered as a consequence. Many local residents, however, were serving as teacher's aides. These individuals found it very difficult to complete their BA degrees and teacher training, because doing so meant moving—for at least a year to 18 months—to a university town. Most felt that they could not afford financially to leave their jobs, and all had family obligations that could not be abandoned.

Researchers LeCompte and McLaughlin convinced the deans of their respective Schools of Education to participate in a partnership between the universities and the school district that would create accelerated programs for aides so that, although they still had to leave the community for a while, they would be able to complete their degrees expeditiously. The partnership included hiring a research assistant with experience in university admissions who evaluated the educational histories of the aides and counseled them as to which courses they needed to take to finish in the least amount of time possible. Unfortunately, one university was unable to provide the special assistance and courses the aides needed; the other, which was located nearby but in an adjoining state, could not grant to the aides in-state tuition or tuition waivers, which made attendance prohibitively expensive. Finally, the district school board failed to grant leaves of absence or sabbaticals to the aides for sufficient time for them to finish their programs. As a consequence, only a few aides participated— and those who did attended a much closer and less rigorous college, one that had not been known for producing well-trained teachers (LeCompte & McLaughlin, 1994).

▰▰▰▰▰

To reinforce the concept of equality among members of the partnership, it is always more effective to base decisions that have negative consequences for members within the project's policy-making body rather than leaving them to the fiduciary agent.

Several steps can be taken before a contract is terminated, such as discussing the source of the problem and providing technical assistance, persuading the partner to provide more supervision or terminate staff, or providing greater cash flow. If none of these attempts is successful, the consortium may agree to terminate a member that violates the principles of partnership.

New organizations may be financially as well as structurally fragile. They may require more maintenance, both financial and technical, than more established organizations. This should not preclude their inclusion in a consortium, but it does suggest that special consideration be given to how many newly constituted organizations can be accommodated without detracting from the viability of the consortium or drawing resources required for the project into the support of the new organization. The Center for AIDS Prevention Studies of the University of California, San Francisco calls upon a nonprofit technical assistance center to assist its community partners. Local community foundations sometimes offer nonprofit organizations technical assistance in the form of workshops and training sessions. A third alternative is to assist smaller nonprofit organizations to identify committed professionals who are willing to serve on their boards of directors and carry out specific technical assistance roles.

Ensuring the Quality of Research in an Action Research Partnership

An action research partnership is defined by both research and action. The partnership must recognize that it

Key point

does not have enough information to constitute a basis for action. A community's need for "more information" drives the work of the action research partnership. *Activists, educators, and administrators should be convinced that information will be useful to their goals.* They must recognize the relative advantages of research, policy assessment, research training, research and demonstration, and evaluation, and they must know how to select among these alternatives when negotiating a project.

Researchers, on the other hand, must have a strong sense of research design and extensive knowledge of research methods in order to know which elements of a project can be negotiated without harming the integrity of the research design, a common concern in community-based research. Because conducting research in local communities can be a sensitive matter, joint development and implementation of research and intervention or program methods is critical to ensuring positive attitudes and positive use, as illustrated in the following case study.

Case Study

The Rapid Sociodemographic Assessment Project: A Regional Research Partnership

Involving communities in demographic research on topics of immediate concern to them has several benefits. First, many states do not implement an interim census. Consequently, after the decade midpoint, organizations and institutions seeking current demographic data on local communities and issues are frustrated in their efforts. Second, community-based organizations do not use what could be available to them because they are unaware of it or are unable to access it. Thus, they react rather than becoming proactive in their efforts to improve conditions in their neighborhoods.

The purposes of the regional Rapid Sociodemographic Assessment project of the Institute for Community Research were to (a) involve community-based organizations and town planning councils in a process of defining, collecting, and analyzing censuslike demographic data, and (b) provide data familiar to these organizations in a format that could be readily used by agency staff for planning and advocacy. The ICR believed that if communities were involved in such a project, they would understand census and other survey data better, be able to critique these data on behalf of their constituencies, and use the data for proactive rather than reactive purposes.

A staff of three researchers under the direction of researcher Marlene Berg undertook to develop relationships with community-based organizations, schools, and other institutions in Hartford's 11 residential neighborhoods and the six towns surrounding the city. Interested organizations were invited to attend instrument planning sessions that involved critiquing and expanding the census short form and developing neighborhood issues questionnaires. Five central agencies received subcontracts to engage in enumeration in their neighborhoods. Staff and neighborhood residents were trained to conduct interviews in these neighborhoods, and they were paid for each interview they returned completed and reviewed. The enumeration and interviewing process introduced agency staff and interviewers to geographic areas and households that they did not know and revealed to them life situations and living conditions that they found challenging and sometimes unacceptable.

The enumeration and interviewing process was conducted in accordance with rigorous standards of excellence in survey research. A stratified sampling strategy was used in which streets in each neighborhood or municipality were enumerated, weighted by density of population, and randomly selected for surveying. One hundred percent of residents on these streets—approximately 10% of the population in each neighborhood and municipality—were interviewed. Interviewers received approximately 10 hours of training. Returned, completed survey forms were checked by ICR researchers and returned to interviewers if found incomplete or inconsistent. Ten percent of all households in each neighborhood sample were revisited as a reliability check. Socioeconomic status, household structure, migration, and other data were analyzed by ICR staff, organized into neighborhoods, and introduced with a history of the neighborhood that was prepared by a public historian with the cooperation of community scholars and indigenous historians.

Community-based organizations in each neighborhood and the six participating municipalities outside of Hartford were asked to coordinate a meeting in their own geographic area to review, discuss, and critique the data and to discuss ways they could be used to improve neighborhood conditions. Thus, the data provided the basis for neighborhood dialogue and coordination. Complete data sets for each neighborhood were organized into user-friendly data files, and guidelines for analysis were prepared so that they could be used in the central agencies. Staff from these agencies, as well as other community users, were trained in the utilization of both the analyzed data and the raw data in these data files. Special issues data requested by each neighborhood were summarized for local use.

This project was useful in introducing survey methods to neighborhood groups and in encouraging dialogue around the uses and limitations of the 1990 census. Furthermore, it served to reduce community suspicions regarding research and researchers, and it brought about requests for partnership in conducting other studies with practical ends. Training researchers to interview in homes in marginalized neighborhoods almost always produces knowledgeable and enthusiastic advocates, and this case was no exception. Some interviewers were teachers, principals, youth work staff, and librarians. Their involvement in interviewing resulted in increased appreciation for their constituencies in ways not met by home visits for problem solving.

━●━●━●━

Identifying a Common Research Problem/ Building the Program Model

Once a working partnership is identified, it must come to consensus on the direction of its work. The group can use the procedures outlined in Book 2 to develop an action research model. Here, we summarize by outlining the steps required to focus a general topic or problem and transform it into a researchable one.

Cross Reference: See Book 2, Chapters 2 and 3, on developing a research project model

- Identify the main problem as the dependent variable

  Participants in the Institute for Community Research's action research training program for women identified abuse of women as the dependent variable domain, and increasing rates of abuse of women as the study problem to be solved. Women in rural villages in Senegal identified female circumcision as the dependent variable, and high rates of reproductive health problems associated with female circumcision as the problem to be solved.

- Identify the causal factors that appear to influence the issue or problem

  Participants discuss the factors that they believe cause the problem, hypothesizing the relationships. This results in a theoretical model negotiated and agreed upon by the group. For example, factors suggested as influencing the abuse of women were pregnancy, financial stress, a high number of young children in the household, and a sick household member.

This generic research/problem-solving process has been used effectively with large groups of community residents, adult women from local neighborhoods, workers in industrial settings (Whyte, 1991), teenagers, international health planners, and youth program planners. In the following example, we demonstrate its role in assisting teenagers to model their research during the 1998 Summer Youth Research Institute.

EXAMPLE 2.20   ━●━●━●━

DEVELOPING THE ACTION RESEARCH MODEL: THE NATIONAL TEEN
ACTION RESEARCH (NTARC) SUMMER YOUTH RESEARCH INSTITUTE

The Summer Youth Research Institute is a program of the Institute for Community Research's National Teen Action Research Institute. The mission of the NTARC is to produce and promote youth-led action research for positive personal, school, and community change. Youth aged 14 to 20 are recruited for the Summer Institute from area schools and paid for their work as research staff of the Institute for Community Research. During the first week of the Summer Institute, teens make a commitment to work in groups in topical tracks. In 1998, the options were either health or education, and the objective in each track was to develop a group research project based on a problem they wished to address through peer education and policy change. To conceptualize their project, teens in both tracks identified a list of problems or issues important to themselves and other teens. From this list, they negotiated to arrive at a single researchable problem. Teens in the education track chose as their problem dropping out of school.

Next, working as a group, they identified the primary factors that they believed were associated with or predictive of dropping out of school. The independent variable domains that they selected were harassment by teachers and students, racism, teen pregnancy, work, drugs, and violence. Hypotheses were constructed linking these domains to the dependent variable, dropping out of school, and connecting one independent variable domain to another. The methods they subsequently selected were designed to validate the hypotheses and, using survey data, to test them (Schensul, 1998, 1998-1999).

Once research partners decide on the central problem and the primary factors associated with it, they can decide to conduct formative research, develop and evaluate an intervention, or evaluate the effects of a policy. The choice of approaches will depend on the skills of the group, the availability and constraints of funding, and the degree to which sufficient information about the situation is determined to exist. Using the tools of research described in Books 2, 3, and 4 of this series, the group must then go on to conduct research and plan for dissemination.

Participants in the project should be involved in all stages of research and dissemination, even if their level of participation varies at each stage of the research. They should receive credit for their contributions by being included in presentations, publications, conferences, and other public events. Failure to adhere to this approach is one of the most common sources of tension and ill will in a partnership. Researchers must keep in mind that contributing to the research model, collecting data, or conducting an intervention for evaluation are as important as writing papers for publication, and these contributions warrant the inclusion of nonresearchers as authors. And interventionists or administrators must keep in mind that reviewing literature, attending research conferences, and publishing are critical to ensuring the flow of research money to the partnership.

Maintaining Stability in Action Research Partnerships

Collaboration in community action research partnerships is not always successful. Community research partnerships (or other partnerships) are likely to run smoothly when the network is stable. Network stability depends heavily on organizational stability. Indicators of organizational stability are the following:

- Experience and familiarity with the topic or problem
- Continuity of administration
- Financial solidarity
- Ability to engage in a conflict resolution process
- Commitment to research as a tool for action

Consortia are only as strong as their individual members. Steering committee members who are experienced directors or appointed substitutes with strong communication skills and a collaborative orientation can address conflicts and miscommunications among consortium members easily. Conflicts occur more readily when representatives are inexperienced. Participants who understand and value data can minimize the inevitable conflicts between research and service. With clear and well-established administrative structures, consortium members can specify how they expect to operate under the consortium structure and can negotiate interagency differences when necessary.

Key point *Significant differences in personnel or institutional policies, operating procedures, and salary levels among consortium members can cause other problems as well.* Different pay scales or benefit packages can result in dissatisfaction among project personnel, who may attempt to seek employment in another consortium organization. The Hartford Community Alliance for AIDS Prevention standardized staff salaries across six organizations to help avoid this problem. In addition, member organizations made the commitment to avoid surreptitious efforts to recruit staff members from one partner agency to new positions in another by offering consortium staff the first opportunity to apply for open positions. This policy also included the agreement to discuss openly implications of cross-hiring for projects and the consortium itself.

Key point *Boards and staff of participating organizations should agree that research is important.* If resistance to research and its uses exists at any level, or if misunderstanding or mistrust occurs, consortium decisions involving data collection, publication, and use are likely to be questioned. Mistrust arising between one organization and the rest of the consortium around the conduct of research will negatively influence the rest of the network and should be addressed immediately. In addition, new organizations are especially susceptible to deploying research staff in other projects because of funding shortages, a practice that can delay progress and trigger interagency conflict.

Conflict among member agencies results in an unstable consortium. One common reason for conflict is inconsistency of internal supervision in participating agencies, resulting in lack of compliance with work requirements. This problem can produce interagency resentments and/or competition and create ill will and lack of cooperation within the consortium. Another common problem results when a participating organization does not take action to retrain, suspend, or terminate an offensive or nonperforming staff member. Situations such as these damage trust, making it difficult to achieve group consensus in the future.

Sometimes, organizations enter consortium relationships without being completely straightforward about their reasons for participating or with different reasons for participating among sectors or departments. Hidden or unknown agendas will appear and may conflict with expressed mutual interests. Occasionally, organizations will participate in partnership planning meetings but then break away to develop their own separate project initiative. Although they may explain their separation as being the result of a difference in perspective, other partnership members may feel the departing organization had a hidden information-gathering agenda.

Additionally, consortia may be damaged when heretofore unknown information about the lead organization is revealed. For example, a lead organization may receive a planning grant to develop a consortium project, whereas other organizations are participating in the planning process only on an in-kind basis. If this information becomes known only after many group meetings have occurred, questions can be asked about the viability of the partnership.

Another problem arises when views and definitions of research differ among consortium members. Issues often addressed by researchers, such as developing conceptual models, the use of comparison groups, sampling and sample sizes, and instrument development and use, may be unfamiliar to service providers in an action research partnership, and they may be reluctant to use them. Joining forces with a Puerto Rican organization serving new arrivals in Hartford, Connecticut, Schensul and her team of researchers were able to use narrative, elicitation, interviews, and focus group research to gather data from mothers and children on activity levels. However, it would not be possible to implement an intervention study with this same organization if it required random assignment of participants into one or more treatment and control groups, because the philosophy of the organization is to offer any and all services to every client.

Qualitative methods other than focus groups may be less acceptable to partners who have learned to value quantitative surveys. For example, a service and policy consortium in Connecticut concerned with the quality of early childhood education included in its 5-year plan a community survey to address problems associated with accessing available day care services, even though a more pressing issue was related to parents' views of the relative importance of early childhood education programs in socializing their children. This latter problem was addressed more easily through ethnographic research. Eventually, after much persuasion, the consortium agreed to use both ethnographic and survey data. Standard measures used to assess programs in a partner institution may not be appropriate to measure the impact of an innovation in that institution. A case in point is the ubiquitous problem of having to use standardized tests in public school education (basic skills tests measuring minimum competency in math, reading, and writing) to assess new, experimental curricula and programs.

An important challenge to consortium building is the need to develop a shared language, set of meanings, and mission for the project. Difficulties in this area may stem from the following:

- Different interpretations of the same conceptual vocabulary
- Lack of understanding of the fundamental vocabulary of the project
- Use of different vocabulary to describe the same concepts
- Discomfort with the project's conceptual framework

It is wise to spend considerable time revisiting the mission of the project and the way it is translated into practice in order to develop and sustain a common vision among consortium members and a common plan for action.

Finally, even when everything is in place and working smoothly, consortia may undergo a process of development, evolution, and decline. Partnerships are subject to external as well as internal conditions for survival and maintenance. Directors may leave, or funding sources may change their priorities or cap their funding in a specific area. Over time, agencies and communities may decide on new directions less consistent with the consortium's mission and purpose. The following case study describes the evolution of a community-based HIV prevention consortium.

The Natural Development, Evolution, and Decline of a Community Research Consortium — Case Study

In 1988, a group of organizations in Hartford organized to plan the first HIV research and prevention program directed toward injection drug users. This consortium—which called itself the AIDS Community Research Group (ACRG) and included the Institute for Community Research, the Hispanic Health Council, the Urban League of Greater Hartford, and the Hartford Health Department—obtained funding from the Centers for Disease Control through the State of Connecticut to conduct a baseline survey of HIV/AIDS knowledge, attitudes, and behavior in Hartford (AIDS Community Research Group, 1988, 1989).

With this experience behind them, the consortium invited two additional organizations to join—a new Latino organization providing services to Puerto Rican and other Latino people with AIDS and their families, and a drug treatment program. The intention of the consortium was to conduct prevention research and test culturally appropriate interventions in culturally situated settings (the Urban League and Latinos/as Contra Sida) and in a culturally neutral site that also offered access to drug treatment programs. The first 3-year intervention study funded by the National Institute on Drug Abuse in 1989 to the consortium through the Institute for Community Research supported the development, implementation, and evaluation of culturally focused interventions at the two sites mentioned above. It also provided support for the incorporation and institutionalization of the Latino agency.

A considerable amount of time and effort was devoted to developing HIV prevention programs at the three service agencies; creating a representative infrastructure for the consortium that ensured equal participation of all agencies in decision making; and consortiumwide understanding of the details of research design. This involved random assignment of participants by self-identified ethnicity, half to a standard intervention at the drug treatment agency and half to a culturally targeted enhanced intervention at each of the two ethnically based service agencies. Men and women were referred to the health department for HIV testing and counseling. Agency services were supported through subcontracts, and research was the responsibility of the Institute for Community Research and the Hispanic Health Council.

This consortium arrangement was referred to as Community Alliance Against AIDS (CAAP). Although it was not without most of the conflicts and dilemmas described herein, the consortium produced effective street recruitment methods; a large sample of injection drug users; and effective approaches to recruiting, assigning, and retaining intervention participants. Success resulted in the award of a second, 5-year study (1993-1997) to the consortium, this time with the Hispanic Health Council as the grantee. Similar to but more comprehensive than the previous study, it also included a standard and an enhanced intervention at the same sites.

The CAAP consortium included member agencies on both sides of the controversy swirling around the introduction of needle exchange programs in inner-city neighborhoods in 1992-1993. Preliminary results of the study convinced agency partners to advocate a needle exchange program in Hartford. Recognizing the potential for resistance in some sectors, the agencies moved to convince first their boards of directors, and then their constituencies. This was especially challenging for the drug treatment program, with its commitment to drug avoidance through treatment rather than HIV prevention through harm reduction—the term used to minimize a significant health risk in an individual without removing the basic cause of the problem. Over time, the consortium was able to convince policymakers and community residents that a needle exchange program would demonstrate reduced risk and increased entry into drug treatment programs, and a needle exchange van was introduced in Hartford. Subsequently, the CAAP consortium decided on the importance of evaluating the needle exchange program and received 3 years of funding from the National Institute on Drug Abuse to do so.

The results of the consortium were significant and included annual local dissemination conferences at which information derived from the studies was shared with local communities and agencies, workshops demonstrating intervention techniques were held, and agencies in the region had the opportunity to share their intervention efforts with others. Agencies and research organizations in the consortium used research results to develop their own research and intervention programs in HIV and drug treatment. In addition, members of the consortium provided ongoing support for a New England HIV/AIDS conference, participated in Ryan White and state planning efforts, advocated harm reduction programs at the national level, and produced more than 30 published articles in professional journals and monographs.

Eventually, changes in staffing, agency direction, federal funding sources, and research needs affected the structure of the consortium. Research organizations in the consortium came to the conclusion that more research was needed to determine how better to reach larger numbers of drug users exposed to HIV, as well as others involved in risky sexual and drug-related behavior. They formed the AIDS Research Consortium (ARC), which now integrates six funded studies. Service organizations were less interested in basic research than service provision. Furthermore, the cost of federally funded research and development efforts was capped, limiting the scope of subcontractual arrangements among agencies. Thus, the financial advantage of working in a large-scale consortium-subcontractual basis deteriorated. Service providers, however, had gained the experience to expand their HIV prevention as a result of their membership in CAAP, and they were able to access more service but not research or evaluation funding.

For all of these reasons, member organizations came to the mutual decision to cease meeting and seeking funding as a consortium and to conduct specific projects with one another in line with individual agency needs. The constituent components of the CAAP consortium remain in place, and every participating organization is financially and structurally sound. The devolution of CAAP has not resulted in its demise, and the relationships among the organizations remain strong and positive. Rather, the current period may be best considered as a temporary lull in the partnership as constituent organizations establish new priorities for themselves and build new working relationships around them.

━●━●━●━

Deciding to Build or Participate in an Action Research Partnership

Action research partnerships offer many interesting opportunities for ethnographers. Roles that could be filled by ethnographers include leadership, chairing working subcommittees, conducting team research or related substudies, training in research methods or group process, evaluation, fundraising and development, and advocacy. Important to keep in mind is that the primary parameter for involvement in any of these activities is the action research agenda of the partnership. Ethnographers are likely to be able to negotiate their own studies only within a well-developed partnership with a broad research program.

We suggest that ethnographers consider the following issues when assessing whether or not to participate in an action research partnership:

- Their desire to contribute to the well-being of the group, the community constituency, and the issues being addressed. Action research is embedded in an action group and a constituency. It is important to demonstrate commitment to both, as well as to the issue.

- Their experience guiding or working with a diverse interdisciplinary group representing a cross-section of researchers, service providers, educators, and community leaders. Good facilitation is critical to moving a group ahead in its search for a project and product. Those who do not have prior experience and facilitation skills may wish to become group members, thus avoiding the responsibility of facilitation and the possibility of making mistakes that delay the progress of the group.

- Their skills in addition to research methods (such as marketing, public speaking and presentations, proposal writing, or team building). Everyone has something in addition to research to offer a partnership. An additional skill enhances an ethnographer's potential to make a contribution.

- Their flexibility (time, patience, and financial security) regarding working toward and waiting for an action research partnership to generate a project. Building action research partnerships takes time because although both have merit, the means (negotiating a project/product) is as important as the end (the resulting project or product).

■ Their home base. Finding an organizational base within the partnership is one way of justifying an ethnographer's presence in the group as well as in one or more of the communities or other settings it is designed to serve.

■ Their desire to publish. In early stages of development, action research partnerships need assistance with literature reviews and collection of both secondary and primary data. In later stages, primary data may be available for analysis and publication. Publication through a research partnership (as with any partnership) calls for joint authorship. This enriches the process of writing and the final publication but is more time-consuming than single authorship. Rules for authorship should be negotiated through partnership leaders as quickly as possible in order to avoid miscommunication and confusion regarding ownership of data.

SUMMARY AND CONCLUSIONS

With the exception of theses and dissertations, most ethnographic research today is conducted in ethnographic, interdisciplinary, action research, or intervention research study teams. This chapter has reviewed the main types of research partnerships in which ethnographers can expect to play important roles. Chart 2.1 summarizes some of the main characteristics of these three different approaches to research partnership.

Conducting research in partnerships is always more complicated than engaging in independent field research. At the same time, ethnographers working alone in the field often find themselves wondering about their right to represent the setting. They search for colleagues with whom to discuss their ideas and share the results of their analyses. They wish for a larger research team in order to investigate more fully the research problem; or they identify new questions important to key informants that a larger ethno-

CHART 2.1 A Comparison of Three Approaches to Building Research Partnerships

Dimensions of Difference in Types of Research Partnerships	Ethnographic Research Teams	Interdisciplinary Research Teams	Action/Applied Research Teams
Purpose/goals	— To conduct team ethnography in local or multiple sites simultaneously	— To conduct interdisciplinary research with ethnography as one element in the study	— To conduct ethnographic research for purposes of solving community problems
Membership	— Ethnographers (may also include students)	— Ethnographers — Researchers from other different social science research traditions	— Ethnographers — Other researchers — Nonresearchers interested in information for problem solving
Types of data collected	— Text data from in-depth and semistructured interviews — Elicitation data — Mapping and network data — Ethnographic survey data — Audiovisual data	— Text data — Elicitation data — Mapping and network data — Audiovisual data — Survey data (ethnographic and nonethnographic) — Psychological, sociometric, epidemiologic data — Biological data (laboratory assays), etc.	— Text data — Elicitation data — Mapping and network data — Service use data — Survey data — Process evaluation data — Outcome data — Cost/benefit data
Intervention?	— Not usually	— Not usually, but may include a theory-guided intervention, often derived from a nonethnographically informed discipline	— Usually a planned intervention; may include — Formative research — Exploratory research — Problem identification — Evaluation

(continued)

CHART 2.1 Continued

Dimensions of Difference in Types of Research Partnerships	Ethnographic Research Teams	Interdisciplinary Research Teams	Action/Applied Research Teams
Challenges	— Overcoming the individualism of traditional ethno-graphic research — Developing comparable cross-site coding categories — Sharing information — Maintaining confidentiality — Maintaining continuing infor-mation exchange across project sites and staff — Deciding on protocols for shared authorship	— Integrating ethnographic and other approaches to research — Triangulating ethnographic and quantitative data — Ensuring equity of ethnographic data and results in informing the study — Developing an interdisciplinary study team language — Maintaining communication across disciplines and project components	— Ensuring presence of all relevant partners — Avoiding domination of research over practice — Developing a common action research agenda in the face of multiple interests — Maintaining partner participation — Managing conflicts among partners — Ensuring partner participation in all aspects of the research — Making sure that research results influence future action
Reasons for choice	— Desire for cross-site problem exploration — Desire for research partners — Enjoy dialogue and exchange — Need stimulation to publish	— Enjoy interdis-ciplinary thinking — See social problems as interdisciplinary — Have interdisci-plinary background — Believe that different approaches to research are complementary	— Desire to use research for social purposes — Enjoy community or organizational development — Interested in testing theory in action — Believe nonresearch-ers can learn to conduct and use research for their own benefit — Like challenge of negotiating appropriate research tools for the setting

graphic research team might have the time and resources to address. Their observations are potentially important in helping communities, schools, and other institutions adapt to new situations. Therefore, invariably, they find themselves drawn to the idea of partnering with local change agents, committees, community leaders, and policymakers.

The intent of this chapter has been to help ethnographers to recognize the advantages of building and joining research partnerships and the many opportunities available to them for doing so. We have also considered and described ways of building and directing research partnerships for investigation and action that ethnographers can create for themselves or with the communities in which they are doing their work. Control over the quality of data collected and use of the data and ethical considerations have been critical to our discussion of each of the three partnerships described in this chapter. We encourage ethnographers to consider different approaches to research partnering and to evaluate both their opportunities and their own preferences. The more complex and action-oriented the partnership, the less control the ethnographer may have over the research. Ethnographers must study the research partnerships they are considering in order to determine which roles are possible and achievable for them, and to what extent their own research interests and styles are a match for the partnership. Over time, a good research partnership of any kind offers ethnographers excellent opportunities for furthering their own as well as their colleagues' research and action agendas.

REFERENCES

Allen, L. (1988). *Otitis media among Puerto Ricans and blacks: Ethnicity, epidemiology and family health cultures.* Unpublished doctoral dissertation, University of Connecticut, Storrs.

AIDS Community Research Group. (1988). *AIDS knowledge attitudes and behaviors survey in a multi-ethnic neighborhood of Hartford: Phase I.* Hartford, CT: Institute for Community Research.

AIDS Community Research Group. (1989). *AIDS knowledge attitudes and behaviors survey in multi-ethnic neighborhoods of Hartford: Phase II.* Hartford, CT: Institute for Community Research.

Bartunek, J. M., & Louis, M. R. (1996). *Insider/outsider team research.* Thousand Oaks, CA: Sage.

Bernal, H., Woolley, S., & Schensul, J. (1997). The challenge of using Likert-type scales with low literacy Hispanic populations. *Nursing Research, 46,* 179-181.

Bernal, H., Woolley, S., Schensul, J., & Dickinson, J. (1999). *Correlates of self-efficacy and self care among Hispanics.* Manuscript submitted for publication.

Bernard, H. R. (1995). *Research methods in anthropology: Qualitative and quantitative approaches* (2nd ed.). Walnut Creek, CA: AltaMira.

Bernard, H. R. (Ed.). (1998). *Handbook of methods in cultural anthropology.* Walnut Creek, CA: AltaMira.

Boas, F. (1948). *Race, language and culture.* New York: Macmillan.

Bronfenbrenner, U. (1977). *The ecology of human development.* Cambridge, MA: Harvard University Press.

Brosted, J., Dahl, J., Gray, A., Gullov, H. C., Hendriksen, G., Jorgensen, J. B., & Kleivan, I. (1985). *Native power: The quest for autonomy and nationhood of indigenous peoples.* Oslo, Norway: Universitetsforlaget AS.

Chambers, E. (1987). Applied anthropology in the post-Vietnam era: Anticipations and ironies. *Annual Review of Anthropology, 16,* 309-337.

Clifford, J., & Marcus, G. E. (Eds.). (1986). *Writing culture: The poetics and the politics of ethnography.* Berkeley: University of California Press.

Crabtree, B. F., & Miller, W. (1992). *Doing qualitative research.* Newbury Park, CA: Sage.

Denzin, N. K., & Lincoln, Y. S. (1994). *Handbook of qualitative research.* Thousand Oaks, CA: Sage.

Dryfoos, J. G. (1990). *Adolescents at risk: Prevalence and prevention.* New York: Oxford University Press.

Eddy, E., & Partridge, W. (Eds.). (1987). *Applied anthropology in America.* New York: Columbia University Press.

Erickson, D., & Stull, D. (1998). *Doing team ethnography: Warnings and advice.* Thousand Oaks, CA: Sage.

Freeman, D. (1983). *Margaret Mead and Samoa: The making and unmaking of an anthropological myth.* Cambridge, MA: Harvard University Press.

Greaves, T. (Ed.). (1994). *Intellectual property rights for indigenous peoples: A sourcebook.* Oklahoma City: Society for Applied Anthropology.

Hawkins, J. D., Catalano, R. F., & Miller, J. Y. (1992). Risk and protective factors for alcohol and other drug problems in adolescence and early adulthood: Implications for substance abuse prevention. *Psychological Bulletin, 112,* 64-105.

Holmberg, A. (1954). Participant intervention in the field. *Human Organization, 14,* 23-26.

Holmberg, A. (1958). The research and development approach to the study of culture change. *Human Organization, 17,* 12-16.

Holmberg, A. (1966). *Vicos: Metodo y práctica de antropología aplicada.* Investigaciones Sociales, Serie: Monografías Andinas, No. 5. Lima, Peru: Editorial Estudios Andinos, S.A.

LeCompte, M. D., & McLaughlin, D. (1994). Witchcraft and blessings, science and rationality: Discourses of power and silence in collaborative work with Navajo schools. In A. Gitlin (Ed.), *Power and method: Political activism and educational research* (pp. 147-166). New York: Routledge.

LeCompte, M. D., Millroy, W. L., & Preissle, J. (1992). *The handbook of qualitative research in education.* San Diego, CA: Academic Press.

LeCompte, M. D., & Preissle, J., with Tesch, R. (1993). *Ethnography and qualitative design in educational research* (2nd ed.). San Diego, CA: Academic Press.

Lee, R. M., & Fielding, N. G. (1996). Users' experiences of qualitative analysis software. In U. Kelle (Ed.), *Computers and qualitative methodologies.* Thousand Oaks, CA: Sage.

Lewis, O. (1966). *La vida.* New York: Random House.

Manderson, L., Kelaher, M., Williams, G., & Shannon, D. (1998). The politics of community: Negotiation and consultation in research on women's health. *Human Organization, 57,* 222-230.

Marshall, P. (in press). Ethical dilemmas in anthropological and epidemiological approaches to prevention research on drug use and HIV/AIDS. In M. Singer & P. Marshall, *Integrating anthropological approaches in epidemiological and prevention research on drug use and HIV/AIDS: Current status and future prospects.* NIDA Monograph.

McGraw, S., Carillo, E., & Schensul, J. (1991). Sociocultural factors associated with smoking behavior by Puerto Rican adolescents in Boston. *Social Science and Medicine, 33,* 1355-1364.

Miles, M., & Huberman, A. M. (1994). *Qualitative data analysis: An expanded sourcebook.* Thousand Oaks, CA: Sage.

Nastasi, B. K., & DeZolt, D. M. (1994). *School interventions for children of alcoholics.* New York: Guilford.

Omidian, P. A., & Lipson, J. G. (1996). Ethnic coalitions and public health: Delights and dilemmas with the Afghan Health Education Project in northern California. *Human Organization, 55,* 355-360.

Pelto, P. J., & Pelto, G. H. (1978). *Anthropological research: The structure of inquiry* (2nd ed.). Cambridge, UK: Cambridge University Press.

Reason, P. (1988). *Human inquiry in action: Developments in new paradigm research.* Newbury Park, CA: Sage.

Redfield, R. (1941). *Folk cultures of the Yucatan.* Chicago: University of Chicago Press.

Schensul, J. (1983). *Otitis media in the Hispanic community* (Policy paper). Hartford, CT: Hispanic Health Council.

Schensul, J. (1996). *Addressing otitis media in the Puerto Rican community: A case example.* Paper presented at the second annual conference of the Puerto Rican Studies Association, San Juan, PR.

Schensul, J. (1998). Community based risk prevention with urban youth. *School Psychology Review, 27,* 233-245.

Schensul, J. (1998-1999). Learning about sexual decision-making from urban youth. *International Quarterly of Community Health Education, 18,* 29-48.

Schensul, J. (in press). Organizing community research partnerships in the struggle against AIDS. *Health Education and Behavior.*

Schensul, J., Donelli-Hess, D., & Martinez, R. (1987). Urban comadronas. In D. Stull & J. J. Schensul (Eds.), *Collaborative research and social change: Anthropology in action.* Boulder, CO: Westview.

Schensul, J., & Eddy, E. (Eds.). (1985). Applying educational anthropology [Special issue]. *Anthropology and Education Quarterly, 16*(2).

Schensul, J., & Schensul, S. (1992). Collaborative research. In M. LeCompte, W. Millroy, & J. Preissle (Eds.), *Handbook on qualitative research methods in education.* New York: Academic Press.

Schensul, J., & Stern, G. (Eds.). (1985). Collaborative research and social policy [Special issue]. *American Behavioral Scientist, 29*(2).

Schensul, S., & Schensul, J. (1978). Advocacy and applied anthropology. In G. Weber & G. McCall (Eds.), *Social scientists as advocates: Views from the applied disciplines.* Beverly Hills, CA: Sage.

Scrimshaw, N. S., & Gleason, G. G. (1992). *RAP: Rapid Assessment Procedures—Qualitative methodologies for planning and evaluation of health-related programmes.* Boston: International Nutrition Foundation for Developing Countries.

Silva, K. T., Schensul, S., Schensul, J., de Silva, A., Nastasi, B. K., Sivayoganathan, C., Lewis, J., Wedisinghe, P., Ratnayake, P., Eisenberg, M., & Aponso, H. (1997). *Youth and sexual risk in Sri Lanka.* Phase II Report Series, International Center for Research on Women, Washington, DC.

Simon, W., Simonelli, J., & Ervin, S. (1998). *Connecting classroom with community: Building effective applied programs for undergraduates.* Workshop on ethnographic field schools given at the annual meeting of the Society for Applied Anthropology, Puerto Rico.

Singer, M., Irizarry, R., & Schensul, J. (1991). Needle access as an AIDS prevention strategy for IV drug users: A research perspective. *Human Organization, 50,* 142-153.

Singer, M., & Snipes, C. (1992). Generations of suffering: Experiences of a pregnancy and substance abuse treatment program. *Journal of Health Care for the Poor and Underserved, 3,* 235-239.

Singer, M., Trotter, R., Marshall, P., Schensul, J., Weeks, M., Simmons, J., & Radda, K. (in press). Ethics, ethnography, drug use and AIDS: Dilemmas and standards in federally funded research. In M. Singer & P. Marshall, *Integrating anthropological approaches in epidemiological and prevention research on drug use and HIV/AIDS: Current status and future prospects.* NIDA Monograph.

Stull, D., & Schensul, J. (Eds.). (1987). *Collaborative research and social change: Applied anthropology in action.* Boulder, CO: Westview.

Weitzman, E. A., & Miles, M. B. (1995). *Computer programs for qualitative data analysis: A software sourcebook.* Thousand Oaks, CA: Sage.

Werner, O., & Schoepfle, M. (1987a). *Systematic fieldwork: Ethnographic analysis and data management* (Vol. 1). Newbury Park, CA: Sage.

Werner, O., & Schoepfle, M. (1987b). *Systematic fieldwork: Ethnographic analysis and data management* (Vol. 2). Newbury Park, CA: Sage.

Whiting, B. W., & Whiting, J. W. M., with Longabaugh, R. (1975). *Children of six cultures: A psycho-cultural analysis.* Cambridge, MA: Harvard University Press.

Whyte, W. F. (1991). *Participatory action research.* Newbury Park, CA: Sage.

Wolcott, H. F. (1995). *The art of fieldwork.* Walnut Creek, CA: AltaMira.

Yoshida, R., Schensul, J., & Pelto, P. (1978). The principal and special education placement. *The National Elementary Principal, 8*(1), 2-4.

INDEX

165

ABOUT THE EDITORS, AUTHORS, AND ARTISTS

Margaret D. LeCompte is Professor of Education and Sociology in the School of Education, University of Colorado at Boulder. After completing her MA and PhD at the University of Chicago, she taught at the University of Houston and the University of Cincinnati, with visiting appointments at the University of North Dakota and the Universidad de Monterrey, Mexico. She also served as Executive Director for Research and Evaluation for the Houston public schools. In addition to many articles and book chapters, she cowrote *Ethnography and Qualitative Design in Educational Research* and coedited *The Handbook of Qualitative Research in Education,* the first textbook and first handbook on ethnographic and qualitative methods in education. As a researcher, evaluator, and consultant to school districts, museums, and universities, she has published studies of dropouts, artistic and gifted students, school reform efforts, and the impact of strip mining on the social environment of rural communities. Fluent in Spanish, she is deeply interested in the education of language and ethnic minority children. She served as a Peace Corps volunteer in the Somali Republic from 1965 to 1967.

Jean J. Schensul is a medical/educational anthropologist. After completing her M.A. and Ph.D. at the University of Minnesota, she conducted intervention research in education at the Institute for Juvenile Research and Center for New Schools in Chicago. She served as cofounder and research director of the Hispanic Health Council in Hartford for ten years, and, since 1987, has been founder and executive director of the Institute for Community Research, based in Hartford, Connecticut, and dedicated to community-based partnership research. She has extensive experience in the use of ethnographic and survey research methods in the United States, Latin America, Southeast Asia, China, and West Africa. Her substantive interests are diverse, reflecting the contributions of ethnography to health, education, the arts, and community development. She co-edited three special journal issues on applied research in education, and policy, and, with Don Stull, coedited a book titled *Collaborative Research and Social Change: Applied Anthropology in Action.* She has published on other topics including substance abuse prevention, AIDS, adolescent development, chronic health problems, and the arts and community building. She is the recipient of a number of National Institute of Health Research grants, immediate past president of the Society for Applied Anthropology, former president of the Council on Anthropology and Education, and recipient (with Stephen Schensul) of the Kimball Award for Public Policy Research in Anthropology. She is Adjunct Professor of Anthropology at the University of Connecticut and Senior Fellow, Department of Psychology, Yale University.

Margaret R. Weeks, a socio-cultural anthropologist, is Associate Director of the Institute for Community Research in Hartford, Connecticut. Her primary interests are in substance abuse and AIDS, development of culturally targeted and gender appropriate HIV prevention for African Americans and Puerto Ricans, and women's issues. Over the past 10 years she has conducted federally funded research in community-based projects in collaboration with other research and service organizations. These studies have focused on documenting and monitoring drug use practices, syringe use, sexual behavior, and health status (including HIV infection) among hidden populations of active heroin and cocaine users, and the studies have utilized a combination of quantitative and qualitative methodologies. A particular focus of her research has been on special issues confronted by women drug users, including risks of sex for money exchanges and the implications of gender and power relations for HIV prevention.

Merrill Singer is a medical anthropologist who specializes in the applied study of inner-city health issues. As the Associate Director and Chief of Research at the Hispanic Health Council in Hartford, Connecticut, and as Associate Clinical Professor in the Department of Community Medicine, University of Connecticut Health Center, he directs or codirects a set of projects that addresses HIV risk among drug users, the relationship between drug use and violence, emergent patterns of drug use, and the role of syringe exchange in HIV risk reduction. He has published more than 100 articles in health and social science journals and as book chapters, and is coauthor or editor of *Medical Anthropology and the World System* (1997), *The Political Economy of AIDS* (1997), *Critical Medical Anthropology*

(1995), and *African American Religion in the 20th Century* (1992). He has served as Chairman of the American Anthropological Association Task Force on AIDS and as a member of the American Anthropology Association Commission on AIDS, the Executive Committee of the Society for Applied Anthropology, the Executive Committee of the National Association of Professional Anthropologists, the AIDS and Behavior Grant Review Committee of the National Institute on Drug Abuse, and the Executive Committee of the Center for the Interdisciplinary Research on AIDS at Yale University. He has also been Associate Editor of the journal *Medical Anthropology.*

Ed Johnetta Miller is a weaver/silk painter/gallery curator/quilter and Master Teaching Artist. Her work has appeared in the *New York Times* and *FiberArts Magazine,* and in the Renwick Gallery of the Smithsonian, American Crafts Museum, and Wadsworth Atheneum. She is the director of OPUS, Inc., codirector of the Hartford Artisans Center, and consultant to Aid to Artisans, Ghana. She teaches workshops on weaving, silk painting, and quilting to children and adults throughout the United States.

Graciela Quiñones Rodriguez is a folk artist, carving *higueras* (gourds) and working in clay, wood, and lithographs with symbols and icons derived from Taino and other indigenous art forms. She builds *cuatros, tiples,* and other Puerto Rican folk instruments guided by the inspiration of her grandfather Lile and her uncle Nando, who first introduced her to Puerto Rican cultural history and Taino culture and motifs. Her work has been exhibited in major galleries and universities throughout Connecticut, at the Bridgeport Public Library, and at the Smithsonian Institution.